Shania Twain

Shania Twain

PETER KANE

UNANIMOUS

Contents

Come On Over

She's been called 'the world's highest-paid lap dancer'. She's been accused of being a studio-made puppet, one who dared not sing live. She's the female Garth Brooks who has been snubbed by the Nashville establishment, who somehow like to imagine her entering into a Faustian pact to sell *their* music down the river. There have been those only too willing to go grubbing around into her past life to find a little dirt to tarnish the squeaky-clean image and clog up those much paraded supermodel pores; the very ones that have won her a multi-million-dollar contract as a Revlon 'spokesperson' alongside the likes of Cindy Crawford, Melanie Griffith, Salma Hayek and Halle Berry.

More bizarrely, word has recently gone round that she has joined the mysterious Sant Mat cult led by one Thakar Singh, aka The Master; a move into the spiritual realm that would require her to forfeit most of life's little pleasures (including alcohol and sex) and 10 per cent of her now considerable fortune. None of this has made the slightest bit of difference. At the beginning of the new millennium, Canada's Shania Twain sits right at the top of the entertainment tree looking down. She's country music's biggest star by miles; an outsider who is responsible for dragging it kicking and screaming out of the 1990s. And as her third album, *Come On Over*, continues breaking records she is looking increasingly unstoppable.

Statistics alone will only ever tell part of the story. But as the first female vocalist to notch up ten million US sales for two back-to-back albums and somebody who

Above On her way to collect six Canadian Country Music Awards. Calgary, September 1998.

it's made all the more remarkable both for the speed and manner in which it has been achieved as well as the fact that, by stealth and subtle reinvention, she has managed to turn that success into something global, conquering large swathes of Europe, Australia and the Far East too.

Barely five years ago, her ascent through the ranks would have seemed like some impossible dream or girlish fantasy. After all, in an age when youth increasingly holds all the aces, for years she found herself being dealt losing hands. Time was ticking away; she seemed to be going nowhere. Yet, just like any good rags-to-riches tale, Shania Twain's story has its very own equivalent of a knight in shining armour rescuing her from likely oblivion and bottomless heartache. As a result, country music has been turned on its head. Songs of temptation, sin, redemption and standing by your feckless man have long gone. The modern, independent country girl knows all about the meaning of the word 'fun' and is fully equipped to go get herself some; not too many questions asked. She also probably grew up watching MTV and is both visually and musically pop, rock and rap literate; as familiar with Stevie Nicks, Van Halen and Dr Dre as, say, Willie Nelson.

Of course, it's all a mighty long way from Kitty Wells' desolate piercing or Patsy Cline

regularly features in men's magazines' polls as one of the world's sexiest women, she's that rare thing, a genuine phenomenon. And

with her ability to 'cry on both sides of the microphone'. Who can imagine either slapping their thigh and expressing a wish to 'Rock This Country!'? These days even legends like Loretta Lynn, Dolly Parton and the late Tammy Wynette have to struggle (and mostly fail) to be heard on the radio. Traditionalists may carp as the banjos get left to gather moss in the backwoods and memories of Hank Williams, Bob Wills, Bill Monroe and the rest fade ever more ghostly into the past, but nothing lasts forever.

Times, attitudes, even morals have changed. So has the music. If it hadn't, country would surely have died or been forever condemned to a marginal, musty, museum-like existence, just like the blues; a heritage tourist attraction housed permanently and creepily in Branson, Missouri, keeping the Osmond family company. Instead, having opened its eyes and ears, it not only lives but also flourishes, attracting a new generation of fans from right across the spectrum. At the forefront, extending the boundaries, and with the likes of Faith Hill and Mindy McCready in pursuit, is Shania. And with *Come On Over* having now overtaken Alanis Morisette's *Jagged Little Pill* as the biggest-selling album ever by a female artist, who would dare say that she hasn't got things right? But, hey, we're getting ahead of ourselves.

Above They don't make them like this anymore. From left to right: Loretta Lynn, Dolly Parton and the late, great Tammy Wynette.

Left Shania showing beyond any reasonable doubt that there's nothing up her sleeves.

If You've Got It – Flaunt It

Toronto: August 8, 1998. It's a beautiful, golden summer's evening beside Lake Ontario. A couple of hours before the gates are even due to open the crowds are out in force, waiting patiently in line; cheery, on their best behaviour, some bearing distinctly home-made banners declaring their affections. Shania is in town playing the second of two sold-out nights at the 16,000-capacity Molson Amphitheatre. Plenty of her family and friends are also here to see her in action, while, backstage, a VH–1 film crew doggedly follow her around. She is two months into what, with customary American lack of restraint, is being billed as her first-ever world tour.

Having just received eight Canadian Country Music Award nominations to go with her recent Country Music Association thumbs up, it's been a pretty good week for her; another in an increasingly long line. What's more, in just over six months, her third album, *Come On Over*, has already clocked up 6.2 million sales, including 760,000 in her native Canada. And now, topping it all off and underlining her myriad achievements to date, there's news in the camp that she is about to become the first country star since Dolly Parton, way back in 1980, to make the prestigious cover of *Rolling Stone*. Things just seem to keep on getting bigger and better for the 32-year-old Canadian.

One of the perks of my own trade is that I occasionally get put on a plane and told to report on gigs for an English music

Above Shania on stage looking suitably poignant, sporting those famous and reassuringly squeaky leather pants of hers.

magazine. As they say, it's a tough job but someone's got to do it. The drill is always the same: bone up a bit beforehand, review the show and snatch a few words with the artist; some possessing fewer words than others, of course. What did I know about Shania Twain? Well, I'd heard the records, seen the videos and read snippets about her in the press. I had worked out she was no replacement Tammy Wynette.

Despite the success of 'Still The One' and 'When in England', Shania was still pretty much an unknown quantity over here at the time. It didn't take a genius to figure out, however, that her style of country music – glossy, sassy, immaculately presented, hooks like claws – owed more to pop and rock than typical modern Nashville fare, never mind the real traditional stuff with its roots in western swing, bluegrass, folk and blues, going right back to the days of The Carter Family and Jimmie Rogers, the Singing Brakeman. Equally obviously, her voice wasn't one of those huge, swollen, ineffably rural, wrist-slitting things that can make hair stand on end and put the fear of God into small children. Nor did it try to be. To my often suspect ears, she sounded like she was more in the Karen Carpenter mould, on the ballads like 'You've Got A Way', at least. As for her much vaunted physical attributes, especially the celebrated and much discussed midriff, let's just say I adhere to the if-you've-got-it-flaunt-it school of thought. Yes, even from a distance of several thousand miles, the pert Ms Twain looked and sounded to be one of the more intriguing musical figures to have come along in quite a while.

I would like to say that, having travelled all the way from London to Toronto for the privilege, she and I spent several enjoyable hours luxuriating in one another's company, fearlessly leaving no subject unturned: politics, religion, love, life, death, hopes, dreams, fears, the usual emotional bric-à-brac; no restrictions, no barriers; both the nitty and the gritty. Alas, I cannot lie. Instead, bounded by etiquette (we were guests after all), myself and photographer Mick Hutson were probably fortunate to be granted 20 minutes of her time (that's probably several thousand dollars' worth at the current exchange rate), less than an hour before she was due to skip on stage in her bouncy platform trainers. Considering she had rather more pressing matters on her mind, like putting on a whopping great show, she turns out to be an exceedingly good sport, even rather frisky.

For the requisite backstage photos she preens and pouts coquettishly; eyes bright, best chest forward, bum wiggling all over the shop, 100-watt smile, an incredibly

Above Animal-loving Shania, always a bit of a sucker for fake-leopardskin prints.

13

game performance turned on as if by a faint snap of the fingers. Patently, the camera loves her; a feeling that, despite her fervent denials, is openly reciprocated. Yet, oddly, it's not sex she oozes so much as healthy, hearty wholesomeness. Many men may fancy her something rotten (and they do, they do), but there is little of the voracious, scarlet-lipped and -nailed predator about her that might alienate the female half of the audience. Cut away all the rigmarole that now inevitably surrounds her and you can still (just) imagine her as somebody you might bump into down the local launderette; appealingly ordinary rather than plain out of reach. Now try imagining that with Jennifer Lopez!

When it came to the chat, I didn't get much beyond lobbing her a few gentle looseners about how was she enjoying life on the road, and her attitude to Nashville and her 'raunchy' image, before time was called. As might be expected from one so well versed in the art of revealing as little as possible about herself, the replies were polite, polished and relentlessly professional. She's done it a thousand times before and since. Small talk has rarely been smaller. Still, we had briefly shared a sofa together, a leather one at that, which meant that each time she shifted her position her leather pants would make a discreet

squeaking noise. I cherish the memory. Wish I'd cleaned my boots, though.

Her performance on stage is no less impressive. Over the course of two hours and kicking off with a feisty 'Man! I Feel Like A Woman!', she works her way through just about everything from *The Woman In Me* and *Come On Over* albums, an amazing 23 songs in total. The voice is strong and true, she's got unlimited reserves of energy and the nine-piece band are drilled with military precision, never dropping a beat. Complete with revolving stage, hazardous amounts of dry ice, flashing lights and plenty of bangs, pops and fizzes, it's entertainment for all the family; slick and fun; hit after hit.

Everything about the show shouts 'big'. It's something that only those at the very peak of their pulling powers would contemplate trying to bring off. But she manages it, and the crowd are on their feet in boisterous approval throughout. By the end of 1999, when the tour finally draws to a halt, more than two million people will have paid to experience Shania live in concert, confirming her as currently one of the hottest acts on the planet. So how exactly did she get here? Given how things started, it's probably a question she still sometimes asks herself. At three in the morning when the rest of the world is asleep, don't we all?

A Girl Called Eilleen

Shania's beginnings were gratifyingly humble; still an important component in the make-up of any self-respecting would-be country artist, a genre in which poorer can often mean better. Sure, times have changed, poverty may no longer be the curse or spur that once drove the likes of the famously impoverished Loretta Lynn or Dolly Parton to seek fame and fortune in Nashville, but it's still a sure-fire way of proclaiming your allegiance to the ordinary, blue-collar folks who are most likely to be buying your records and attending your shows.

If you could claim that you were one of twenty children, lived in a two-room shack, walked barefoot to school every day and were grateful for your strict diet of bread and water, so much the better. You may have been dirt poor but you were happy, or so the stories tend to go, grateful for even the most meagre of mercies shining an occasional warming light on your otherwise pitiful childhood existence. Success, if it comes, is reckoned to be simply the result of making the most of your allocated talents. It is never to be taken for granted. These are the sort of roots that are supposed to go deep enough to help keep feet somewhere near the ground and heads out of the clouds. As a star, you forget all this at your peril because, rest assured, your public won't.

Her present million-dollar lifestyle in a Swiss chateau could hardly be further away from how Shania first started out on this earth, yet these are lessons that she has

plainly learned inside out. With almost
every public utterance she goes to quite
extraordinary lengths to paint herself as a
simple girl from the backwoods, one who
has somehow managed to clamber over all
the obstacles put in her way without ever
once forgetting her past. Give her an axe or
a chainsaw, it appears, and she can chop
down a tree; hand her a snare to set and it's
farewell Mr Rabbit – or at least it would be
if she were still that way inclined and not
the animal-loving vegetarian of today. What

has emerged is a convincing self-portrait of
somebody who has come to recognise the
value of her tough raising and who, beneath
the soft-seeming exterior, is clearly a woman
who knows exactly how to look after herself.
She is certainly nobody's appendage or just
another vacuous pretty face. There again,
she had an early start and was never
permitted such a luxury.

The bare bones of Shania's earliest years
are that she was born Eilleen Regina
Edwards (her professional name would only

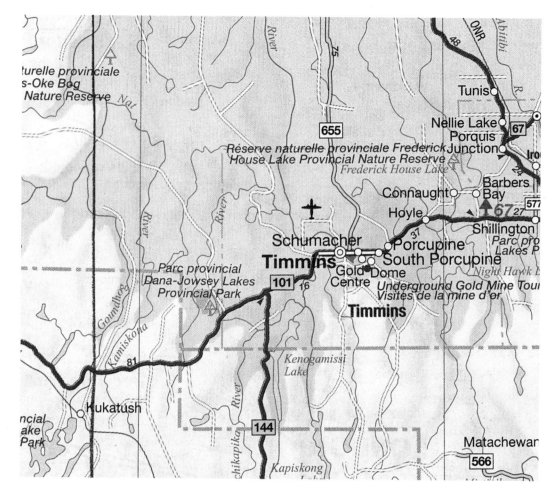

come much, much later) on 28th August, 1965 in Windsor, Ontario; a functional city on the other side of the river from Detroit, just across the Canadian border. She was the second of Clarence and Sharon Edwards' three daughters; Jill being the eldest and Carrie-Ann bringing up the rear. Clarence was of French-Irish stock and worked as a railroad engineer, an occupation that, in theory at least, quivers romantically with the notion of one of American music's most enduring themes, that of restlessly moving from town to town, of hopeful escape and eternal renewal. The reality was that young Eilleen's parents were already swiftly growing apart. Not long after the birth of Carrie-Ann, and with Eilleen aged just two, they went their separate ways, divorcing a couple of years later. Sharon took custody of the girls and Clarence quickly dropped out of sight, playing no discernible part in the future raising of his children. Not surprisingly the adult Shania has few memories of her natural father.

Rather than hanging around in Windsor waiting for something, anything, to happen, Sharon decided that a fresh start might be the answer; easier said than done when you've got limited marketable skills, next to no money and a clutch of young kids in tow. After some false starts, she eventually settled on Timmins, Ontario, a sprawling

Above Another big show coming up. Backstage at Toronto's Molson Amphitheatre, August 1998.

pleasingly temperate climate, anyway. During the winter months (October to April or thereabouts in that part of the world) the thermometer can easily drop to 30 degrees below zero. Add on the wind-chill factor and you can maybe double that figure; cold enough to make even a snowman shudder and think about putting on an extra layer of thermal underwear. Mother Nature calls the shots and nobody bothers arguing. Still, there's always the possibility of ice fishing out on one of the hundreds of nearby lakes to help pass the time.

Timmins, which isn't shy of calling itself 'the gateway to the North Eastern Arctic and Greenland', might sound like a freezing version of the back of beyond, but it's a tough, proud working community built upon the munificence of the surrounding area's unfeasibly rich mineral deposits, including gold. With its churches, bars and regulation civic amenities it's not a whole lot different from hundreds of similarly sized towns spread across the American continent. The local Kidd Creek mine is even reckoned to be the largest producer of zinc and silver in the world. Today, though, it's far more likely to be known as the hometown of one of the planet's real musical superstars. After all, this is where the plain-sounding Eileen Edwards grew up, went to school and first started stretch-

town of some 40,000 souls in the east of the province, 400-odd miles north of Toronto. It's not exactly the kind of place that would come near the top of many lists; well, not if you're after glamour, bright lights and a ing her vocal chords in public. In 1996, in recognition of her achievements, she was given the keys to the town and had part of the local highway named after her. Suffice to say that nobody would have predicted that kind of reception even ten years ago, never mind when she was first starting out. Timmins people aren't generally the kind to go make waves.

Having made the decision that the town was a suitable spot to raise her children, life for Sharon quickly took a turn for the better when she met,

Above A small person made happy as thousands look on. Another long afternoon of cramp-inducing pen-wielding for the highly fan-conscious Shania.

fell in love with and eventually married Gerald Twain, a union that would later produce sons Mark and Darryl. Jerry was a full-blood Ojibwa Indian and brought to the relationship and newly formed family unit the wisdom and rich cultural heritage of this ancient, if little-known, tribe. By legally adopting Eilleen, Jill and Carrie-Ann as his own, this also meant that from then on the three young sisters were full members of the Temagami Anishnawbe Bear Island First Nation. In fact, irrespective of her bloodline, Eilleen was now officially recognised as 50 per cent North American Indian. These were proper roots, ones to be proud of and, since her fame, Shania has celebrated them accordingly; a little too zealously, some would later claim.

Still, perhaps it's little surprise that memories of childhood weekends and summers spent on the Matagami Reserve with her freshly

'I wasn't a girlie kid … It's not in my nature to be girlie even now.'

Left Going up in a puff of smoke? In action at Air Canada Centre, Toronto, March 1999.

inherited grandparents should, with constant retelling, have acquired an almost golden hue. 'At the time it was a very communal style of living,' she explained to *Q* magazine's John Aizlewood. 'It's very different now, but back then, everybody still mostly lived in outhouses with a little pee-pot on the porch. You could sleep pretty much where you wanted and go eat at anyone's house like it was all one big family. It wasn't like you were visiting your grandmother so you had to stay with her. There were no formalities at all.' A bit of a tomboy by her own admission ('I wasn't a girlie kid … It's not in my nature to be girlie even now'), at eight Eilleen could use a rifle and set an animal trap. 'I was a good shot with a bow and arrow,' she confirmed to Robin Eggar of the UK newspaper the *Mail On Sunday*. More importantly, she got to learn the meaning and importance of 'family', its worth and responsibilities.

Life for the Twains in their three-bedroom clapboard home, though, was mostly as hard as the surrounding terrain. Regular jobs were never easy to come by and money was tight and forever an issue. While Sharon, prone to bouts of depression, often stayed home to look after the little ones, Jerry took what work he could get as a logger in the surrounding forests. He was a proud man whose pride even dictated that he would

rather his family went without than him claiming dole; to turn to public assistance would be, he felt, a painful admission of his failure to provide for them. Inevitably the ends sometimes refused to meet. With seven mouths to feed, meat was a luxury; hunted moose on the dinner menu was a cause for much rejoicing. Often there was just bread, milk and sugar on the table, with sandwiches smeared only with mustard or

Above Mind your back. Caught from behind at 1995's Billboard Awards in New York.

mayonnaise filling the growing stomachs of the Twain clan during their school lunch breaks. Then there was the cold, lots of it. 'There were many days when we had to huddle round the stove because we couldn't pay the heating bill. We went to bed wearing our coats, literally freezing. It's not the way you want to live – you can die in those conditions. I don't think our parents would have allowed us to die, they would have taken us to a shelter, but we definitely endured what we could, we pushed it to the limits. We managed and I'm glad we did. A little bit of hardship's OK, it's not the end of the world, it's better than being abused,' is how Shania now puts it.

Poor though Eilleen and her family may have been, it soon became clear that the youngster possessed something money can never buy: a genuine musical talent. From an early age she was not only confidently dispatching nursery rhymes of the 'Twinkle Twinkle Little Star' variety, but making up her own sweet-voiced little ditties too, entertaining herself for hour after hour, having quickly picked up the rudiments of guitar from Jerry, a capable self-taught strummer. So tickled by her daughter's abilities was Sharon that the fledgling star's first public appearance took place when, aged three, she was plonked by her mother on top of the counter at a local diner to

entertain the patrons by singing along to the jukebox. In first grade at school she even managed to earn herself the mocking nickname of 'Twang', after a typically effusive rendition of the Olivia Newton-John crossover country-pop hit 'Take Me Home Country Roads' during a show-and-tell session. Sadly, it also meant her classmates had already marked her cards as a show-off, somebody with ideas above her station. 'From that point on, I was afraid to perform,' she confessed back in 1994 to Canada's *Country Music* magazine. She retired, hurt, to the safety of her bedroom. Not that she would stay there licking her wounds for long. She wasn't allowed to.

Sharon, in particular, was convinced she had a bona fide prodigy on her hands. She would do everything in her powers to encourage Eilleen; an opportunity, perhaps, to realise some of her own long-burnt-out dreams through her offspring and provide some sort of hope for the Twain family's future too. 'I think my mother's obsession for my music kept her going a lot of the time. We'd come home from school, she'd still be in bed. She would get very depressed. She would get up and want to hear my songs. Then she would get on the phone and start working out where I was going to sing. It was her saving grace,' Shania told the TV music station VH-1's *Behind The Music*

programme. From a distance, however, the encouragement might just as easily be read as pushing a little too hard, placing an unsuitably heavy burden on a pair of very tender shoulders. Well before hitting her teens, Eilleen was being sent out to sing for her supper in the kind of places that children would never normally be allowed to venture anywhere near, never mind perform in. Kitted out like a pocket-sized cowgirl in frontier buckskin and denim, clutching a guitar almost as big as herself – 'I was so small that they couldn't lie flat on

Above 'What do you mean, Faith Hill's taller?' In-store signing session. Brockport, New York, December 1998.

Far left A big smile for the camera during the Amnesty International Gala. Paris, December 1998.

'I liked to escape my personal life through my music. Music was all I ever did.'

me' – it's an experience she admits scared her half to death. Small wonder.

Community centres, family get-togethers, local fairs, Eileen would tackle them all. At an old folks' home where her great-grandfather was resident she found herself singing for an audience, half of whom complained she was too loud, while the other half moaned about not being able to hear a damned thing. She was earning her stripes the hard way, learning how to hold the attention of a crowd; all valuable training for the future, of course. One of the toughest gigs of all was Timmins' Matagami Hotel, where her mother worked occasional nights in the kitchen. Being a minor, she was only allowed on stage once they had stopped serving liquor – at midnight. By then the air would be thick with the smoke and sour whiskey fumes from a crowd of hardened working men who had come to relax and let off a little steam and who had nothing much to rush home to; a thought to send even the most seasoned performer scuttling for the toilet in terror. But with her parents proudly looking on, armed with Dolly Parton's tear-jerking 'To Daddy' ('Mama never wanted any more than what she had, if she did she never did say so to daddy'), Kris Kristofferson's 'Me And Bobby McGee' and the like, she would battle through, this tiny kid regaling the crowd with tales of love, loss and disappointment way beyond her possible understanding. You don't tend to forget those kind of experiences.

'I pretty much missed my childhood,' Shania admitted to *Cashbox*, looking back on those times. 'I've always been focused. My career has always been very consuming. It probably consumes me less [now] than it did as a child. I liked to escape my personal life through my music. Music was all I ever did. I spent a lot of time in solitude with just my guitar, writing and singing for hours. I would play till my fingers were bruised and I loved it. But I never enjoyed the pressure of being a performer. My parents forced me to perform which, in the long run, was the best thing because I was naturally quite a recluse. If not for my parents, I'd still be singing in my bedroom.' Use of the word 'forced', with its undeniable whiff of third-world child-slave labour and scrawny kids being shoved up Dickensian chimneys, was something that she would later admit was a tad unfortunate. Not that the reality was anything other than harsh.

Having been packed off to bed at a sensible time in the evening, Eilleen would be woken around the witching hour and then, in the blistering cold, be taken to her place of work at the Matagami or somewhere similar. 'I'd get up and sing a few songs with the band and before I knew it I was actually doing clubs professionally. From the age of eight, I was doing weekends, the odd gig here and there. I did everything my parents could get me on,' she says. Equally surprisingly, perhaps, the education authorities didn't seem to mind either. 'The school knew what I did and were very supportive. They knew how serious I was about my music and they didn't have any major problems with that. Not that I advertised the fact. I didn't go to school saying, Hey, I was in a bar until two this morning.' Besides, what real use were top grades and a hatful of qualifications to Eilleen when it was already clear that a career in music was her dream, and maybe

her destiny? She already knew that what she wanted more than anything in the world was to be one of Stevie Wonder's backup singers.

Sharon, most of all, never had any doubts about what her daughter could achieve. 'She knew I was talented and she lived with the hope that my abilities were my chance to do something special,' confirms Shania. That unshakeable faith would come in handy over the years ahead.

Above Taking time out from VH-1-sponsored *Divas Live!* concert. New York, April 1998.

Far left In rehearsal, New York City, August 1997. It's okay, that's not a cardigan she's wearing.

One Of The Guys

By the age of twelve, the musically obsessed Eilleen was already a stage veteran. If, in private, her listening habits ranged from Tamla Motown to the honey-coated pop of the Carpenters and the soothing Californian harmonies of The Mamas And The Papas, in public she would sing only country songs. After all, this was the music that Sharon and Jerry knew, understood and liked best; Willie Nelson, Waylon Jennings, Tammy Wynette, the usual names. There was a practical reason too: a steady stream of work was readily available; 20, sometimes 25 dollars a night, cash in hand.

The rest of the world may not know it, but Canada takes its country music very seriously, boasting its own well-established scene. Though a mighty long way from Nashville on the map, once you get away from the border cities, out into the wilds and the scattered townships, it's the everyday musical choice of the ordinary rural working men and women. The reasons are clear: a shared identity with the core values of family, home and Mother Earth that traditionally underpin many of the songs; the common language and the same cultural roots too – English, Scottish and Irish. Of course, hailing from Kentucky or Tennessee will always sound more authentic and look better on the C.V. But as Hank Snow, Anne Murray and Michelle Wright have shown over the years, being a Maple Leafer doesn't mean automatic disqualification from acceptance below the 49th parallel, even if there is a tendency to

Above, above right and above far right Nashville queens Tammy Wynette and Dolly Parton plus the man who kick-started it all, Hank Williams.

be regarded as 'seconds', not quite the genuine article. Somebody with first-hand experience of the business higher up the ladder than the Twains was Mary Bailey. And the first time she heard Eilleen sing was a key moment in Shania's story.

Mary was a red-headed regular on the Canadian country-music circuit who, despite some national success with a tune called 'Mystery Lady', was fast resigning herself to a life out of the spotlight. In 1978 in Sudbury, Ontario she happened to be standing by the side of the stage, waiting her turn to go on, watching the twelve-year-old Eilleen go through her act. She was

overwhelmed by what she saw and heard — literally so. Tears started to well up in her eyes, something was tugging on her heartstrings and her brain was telling her this eerily confident child was already a class apart; perhaps even, in time, the very star that she now knew she would never be herself. The song that really triggered it was the old Hank Williams number, 'I'm So Lonesome I Could Cry'. Few have ever got near to matching Williams' gift for expressing utter human desolation quite so economically, and with its beautifully simple melody and lines like 'I've never seen a night so long when time goes

crawling by/The moon just went behind the clouds to hide its face and cry', it touches depths that most songwriters can only dream about reaching. Mary knew that the youngster was not just prettily trilling the words; she was living them like she had been there. After the show she spoke with Sharon, as ever the chaperone and flag-waver. She told her how moved she had been by her daughter's performance and how, maybe, she could help her. They agreed to stay in touch.

Back in Timmins, Eilleen continued working her socks off, playing wherever she could, including local TV and radio stations. She also found time to blow a little trumpet in the school band ('I was never very good at it') and dealt burgers and fries in the local McDonald's, another valuable life experience by all accounts. 'I learned there's a certain work ethic and a certain discipline that goes with working there because they're so strict on their consistency. There's an etiquette you have to have when dealing with the public. It's a good discipline,' Shania has since explained. In 1982, aged 16, she graduated from Timmins High and Vocational School. She was considered a serious, self-contained young woman with drive and

Above Mary Bailey, a minor Canadian country star herself, who first spotted the pre-teen Shania doing a suitably plangent version of 'I'm So Lonesome I Could Cry' in 1978. She would later become Shania's friend, mentor and first manager.

Left At the London premiere of the movie *Notting Hill*, 1999.

Below right With Pat Boone at 1997's US Music Awards.

ambitions way beyond those of her peers. In the class yearbook of a friend she wrote, 'Remember me when I'm famous and I'll remember you.'

Never afraid of hard graft, she had also been helping Jerry out in his small, newly established reforestation business which had been set up with the aid of a government grant designed specifically to assist Native American Indian enterprises. As ever, she got stuck right in, as an extract from her biog for the *Country Music Encyclopaedia* tells: 'I was a foreman with a 13-man crew, many of whom were Indians. I'd run the crew and we'd plant through the summer. We'd get up between four and six in the morning, live on beans, bread and tea, walk to up to an hour to the site and work there all day with no shelter in rain, snow or sunshine, in the middle of the bush, hours from civilisation. I did that for five years. It was very hard work, but I loved it.' To *Q* magazine she confessed, 'I was one of the guys, I really was. I worked as hard as any of them, if anything harder. I was determined never to be outwalked or outworked and I gained tremendous respect from my workers.'

See a picture of Shania now, of course, and it's all but impossible to imagine her ever being considered 'one of the guys', or that, as she claims, people often mistook

'I was one of the guys, I really was.'

'I saw at school that if you had breasts and you bounced and you were feminine, that everyone paid attention only to that. I hated that.'

her for a boy, even in her teens. Yet rather than celebrating her growing womanhood, she initially resented it. 'I saw at school that if you had breasts and you bounced and you were feminine, that everyone paid attention only to that. I hated that,' she told *Country Weekly* magazine. Such self-consciousness about her developing body, however, could not last long if she was serious about her chosen career – and she was. Besides, hiding behind a curtain or dressing like a house-bound frump was never likely to be an option, was it? Even today, though, with all the apparent sexual confidence she exudes on stage, she's got a thing about her legs: 'stocky' and 'athletic', she reckons.

In 1983, shortly before finishing high school, Eilleen took a fresh musical path. Having been spotted performing on a local TV telethon, she threw in her lot with a neighbourhood rock band. 'We wore black satin jackets with our logo on the back. We were called Long Shot. We were pretty good actually, pretty dangerous for my hometown and pretty popular. The bars we played in would have to lock the doors at 9pm – before we came on stage – because the places would be so full. And I wasn't even legally old enough to be in the bars. We would mix stuff like Crosby, Stills, Nash and Young with pop-rock Foreigner-type stuff. And we'd do stuff by A Flock Of

Seagulls,' she recalled to *FHM* magazine in the UK. As it turned out, Long Shot might have been better called Short Shot. Musical differences were soon cited and the members went their separate ways despite a sturdy reputation throughout Ontario. Eilleen simply took it all in her stride, another notch on her performing belt.

By this time, Mary Bailey was also back in the picture – as Eilleen's manager. Sharon had rung to enlist her help, knowing that Mary's contacts would be invaluable. She also trusted Mary and knew she shared her bottomless faith in her daughter. Having recently said goodbye to her own singing career, Mary was only too happy to do what she could. In Eilleen, she thought she saw something of the young Tanya Tucker (country music's Lolita figure during the 1970s), that little extra sparkle that separates the blessed from the merely good. A trip to Nashville was arranged. Eilleen was shown around and tested out. But the fish refused to bite and the pair returned home empty-handed. For all her belief, Mary was not totally convinced that, aged 18, Eilleen was 100 per cent committed to trying to make it as a country star. They shook hands and parted, leaving the door ajar for whatever the future might hold.

Despite the strength of her family ties, it was unlikely that fame would ever come searching for Eilleen Twain in Timmins. She would therefore have to go looking for it someplace else. Toronto, the nearest big city, with a bustle all of its own and Canada's entertainment capital, fitted the bill nicely. During the mid-1980s Shania spent three years there hustling for whatever work she could get, whatever paid the rent. To keep the landlord off her back, she had a day job doing secretarial work. But the hunger for success was as strong as ever, driving her through all sorts of performing hoops. Sometimes she got the chance to sing her own songs; mostly she sang somebody else's – rock, pop,

Above You can see why Revlon wanted Shania to be one of their spokespersons, can't you?

Far left Shania holds back the crowds at the New York State Fair, July 1998.

country, r 'n' b, cabaret, it didn't matter. She was nothing if not versatile, flexible. Occasionally, there were even small triumphs, like the time she got to open for Broadway musical star Bernadette Peters. For all her determination and professionalism, though, the big break never arrived. Ever the smalltown girl, she would return regularly to Timmins to help out Jerry's tree-planting business. Then, 'after a summer of northern exposure, from treacherous June blackflies to an August hailstorm, I'd go back to Toronto and slip into my sequinned gown again,' Shania remembers.

This particular chapter in her life, however, was to end suddenly and tragically on 1 November 1987. Shania was back in Toronto. Early in the morning – it was a Sunday – the phone rang. A flatmate answered it. Shania immediately sensed something was wrong. 'My heart was just jumping out of my chest,' is how she describes the feeling of enveloping panic. At the other end of the line was Jill, her sister. She had some bad news, far worse even than Shania could have feared. Her mother and father were both dead, killed outright when their vehicle was hit head-on by a logging truck on the way back from one of their reforestation sites up country. The sense of utter desolation and loss are almost impossible to imagine. For a tightly knit unit such as the Twains, it hit doubly hard. Even when times were at their bleakest, Sharon and Jerry had always been there for their kids. Their love was unquestioned. They were the reason why Shania had always kept faith in her own abilities. Now, out of the blue, they were gone, ripped away. 'When you hit an emotional bottom like that and come face to face with the fragility of life and how fleeting it can be, then you realise how nothing else matters and your priorities completely change,' she reflected, a decade later.

Amid all the grieving, there was another matter that needed to be sorted too: who was going to look after Daryl and Mark? Logically, there was only one candidate: Shania. Jill already had a home and family of her own. 18-year-old Carrie-Ann wasn't much more than a kid herself, certainly not equipped to look after two teenage boys. 'Somebody had to do it. Shania is very strong and strong-willed,' explained the youngest sister to VH-1. It was just as well. She needed to be. Aged 21 and back once more in Timmins, she was precisely where she started, only now she had not only lost the two most important people in her life, she was the de facto head of a family, too. 'It was like being thrown into the deep end of a pool and just having to swim,' was the

analogy she used in *People*. A lesser individual might have buckled under the strain. There was a good chance she could have kissed goodbye to her career right there and then. But Shania was raised as a fighter, a doer. She wasn't about to let all her hopes simply vanish without putting up some resistance. She contacted her old friend and former manager, Mary Bailey, for guidance.

Mary didn't muck around. She sent a demo tape of Shania to the producer of a glitzy, legs-and-feathers Las Vegas-style revue at a resort called Deerhurst in Huntsville, less than three hours by road from Toronto. It proved promising enough to earn her an audition, leading immediately

Above Shania sports a sort of gypsy/ethnic look in this early shot. Still a bit of work to be done on the image by the look of things.

Far left At the 1999 CMA Awards show and an all-too-rare sighting of her legs. Not bad, are they?

to a job offer as a featured singer. Now Shania had work for herself, some much-needed stability and a way of keeping her family together. For three years, eleven shows over six days a week, it became her world and another important element of her tough education, even requiring her to learn to dance a little. She was part of a big production where everything had to be done exactly on cue, the same each night, knocking out everything from Motown medleys to Andrew Lloyd Webber lung-busters with the maximum pizzazz and minimum offence for audiences of tourists and conference delegates more interested in eating, boozing and carrying on a conversation. Yet Shania made them sit up and listen. She was good, really good, better than they deserved.

For such a creative, naturally independent spirit it must have often been a soul-shrinking experience. Behind the mask and outward glamour, there were inevitably times when she really didn't want to be there on stage, under the piercing lights, the focus of attention in her slinky green gown, belting out Judy Garland's 'Over The Rainbow' where, conveniently, 'troubles melt like lemon drops.' If only. In reality she was lumbered with all the worries of a

38

woman, a parent, twice her age. 'It was a very emotional, tragic time. Picking up the clothes in their [her brothers'] rooms was the least of my worries. I was more worried about drugs, alcohol, AIDS, pregnancy, all those things,' she told the *Sunday Mirror* magazine in the UK. More than once the thought crossed her mind that, maybe, this was about as good at it would get. She bought a house, a family truck and settled down, possibly for good.

As an indication of what Shania got up to musically away from Deerhurst during this period, in late 1999 some previously unreleased tracks she had recorded a decade earlier found their way into the shops. Called *Beginnings: 1989–90* (alternatively *Wild And Wicked* in the UK) and credited to Eilleen Shania Twain, the CD consists of songs she wrote and recorded with a California-based guitarist called Paul Sabu (son of 1930s and '40s child film star, Sabu 'The Elephant Boy'; what a strange, small world it sometimes is) and features her in full rock-chick mode, including a version of Cher's 'Half Breed'. Naturally, Shania wasn't best pleased. 'This is not the way I want people to hear my music,' she has complained. Suffice it to say it's fascinating as a historical document, but a mighty long way from what lay around the corner.

By the summer of 1991, though, with her siblings' schooling complete and her sisterly duties almost done, the clouds finally began to lift over Shania's life. In a press release issued years later she described the feeling: 'When they left, I felt like a 45-year-old woman whose kids had gone away to college. I was like, "Wow! I have my whole life to live now." I had all this time on my hands. I didn't have to cook and clean for anybody. Didn't have to pay any bills but mine. Didn't have to go to school meetings. Didn't have to pick them up after work and take them to teen dances. Drive them here. Drive them there. It was like, "I'm free!" I said, "Now what am I gonna do with my life?" I decided I wanted to go for it.'

And she did.

'I said, "Now what am I gonna do with my life?" I decided I wanted to go for it.'

Nashville Beckons

Shania might well have told herself that she was now ready for one more, perhaps final, assault on the citadel of fame, but how exactly? Clicking your fingers is always a cheap and simple option; a pity it never works. One person who did not need any convincing, though, was her manager and mentor, Mary Bailey. Mary didn't possess a magic wand either, nor was she one of the recognised music-business big-hitters, yet she did have 100-per-cent belief in her protégée, some useful contacts and an enviably solid reputation as a fair player in country-music circles.

Newly enthused by what potentially lay ahead, one of Mary's first tasks was to encourage a change of name. Eilleen Twain, after all, was hardly a handle to set pulses racing or likely to be celebrated in lights. Where was the glamour, the sex, the aroma of exoticism? A compromise was duly reached: in memory of her parents, the family name could stay, provided the Eilleen part didn't. As luck would have it, the answer turned out to be right there in front of everybody. One of the wardrobe mistresses at Huntsville happened to be called Shania. As names go, it had the lot; scarcity value, slightly mysterious and almost musical when pronounced correctly; beautiful, in other words. Better still, it was an Ojibwa Indian name. Better than that, and unknown to Shania at the time, it meant 'I'm on my way'. Now, if ever there was a sign …

Newly christened and with a fresh sense

Above Testing: one, two, one, two. Shania in full dress-rehearsal mode.

of purpose, of hope, Shania handed in her notice at Deerhurst. Guided by Mary, the plan was to return to Timmins in preparation for another tilt at Nashville. Maybe now things would finally start to fall into place. Mary had already been busy pulling a few strings. She had sent a new demo tape of Shania to an old acquaintance of hers, Dick Frank, a Nashville music lawyer, and kept pestering him until he agreed to take a weekend trip to Huntsville with his wife to run an experienced eye over Mary's client just before she bade farewell

to the resort. Once the legal representative of, among others, the sainted Patsy Cline, Frank's opinion carried plenty of weight in Music City. What's more, he had the keys to unlock more than a few doors. Witnessing Shania first hand and being suitably bowled over, he was in no doubt he could bring some of that influence to bear in helping to secure her a record deal. Impressively, Frank turned out to be as good as his word.

Aged 26 and back in Timmins once more, awaiting the phone call that promised to put her career right on track, Shania took a job behind the complaints desk at Sears. She was also, by then, having a romantic fling with a guy called Paul Bolduc, which must have been pretty serious because she later described him as her 'saving grace' on the liner notes to her debut album. Not only that, but Paul's mother was a co-founder of Shania's Canadian fan club and, for a while, ran the operation out of the basement of the family home. Yet, for whatever reason, the liaison didn't last.

In truth, Shania's love life has always been a bit of a mystery, a black hole, to anyone on the outside. Rather than a well-marked trail of badly broken hearts in keeping with her current status as one of the world's most eminently desirable women, there are only gaps and blanks during her years of singledom; precious little to shatter the healthy, wholesome, almost girl-next-door image she projects in sharp contrast to the apparently voracious Madonna, say, or the barely licit teenaged writhings of new kids on the block like Britney Spears or Christina Aguilera. Shania herself has coyly claimed she was always far more interested in advancing her own career than dating a succession of men who would have to be content playing first reserve to her guitar and her aspirations. As for the intricacies of any past relationships, she simply chooses not to tell. So be it. Whatever, Shania was soon to leave this old life of hers – and Paul – behind forever.

Back in Nashville, Dick Frank set to work stirring up some interest in his latest musical 'find'. One of the people he approached was Norro Wilson. Wilson was Music City through and through, a seasoned independent writer-producer and even sometime singer who had notched up a few minor country hits of his own during the early 1970s. More importantly, having helped pen the odd song or two for the likes of Charlie Rich and Tammy Wynette and, over the years, overseen successful sessions for Charley Pride, Ray Price and Oklahoman diva Reba McEntire, he knew his onions. Wilson agreed to put together a cheap three-track demo as a showcase to be touted around the major labels. With Mary

Bailey helping to foot the bills, Shania was flown south for the recording and, almost before anybody knew it, a deal was struck with Mercury-Nashville. It was all fixed; the girl from little old Timmins was finally going to be a star, just like Sharon and Jerry always believed she would. Everybody at the record label, from company president Luke Lewis down, was convinced of it. Nothing could stop her now. Or could it?

Shania quit her 9 to 5 at Sears and moved down to Nashville. As well as the recording sessions she needed to be groomed too.

Above Back home in Timmins when it's 30 degrees below zero, all the girls dress like this.

Top Saturday night at the Grand Ole Opry, Nashville.

Above Nashville's Ryman Auditorium, country music's spiritual home since 1943.

There were suddenly promotions, publicity, photo shoots, interviews and future videos to think about. How should she look? What should she wear? What image did she want to project? What, precisely, was to be her appeal, her uniqueness, the special something that would make people buy her records? After years spent hovering around the outer edges of the music business she was finally being invited into the inner sanctum to partake in all that was on offer, gold card in hand. Thousands of dollars would be lavished on her, marketing her in order to satisfy others' wants and needs. There was just one catch: in return she would have to do pretty much as she was told. And if the untried Shania, this complete unknown from the Canadian backwoods, initially entertained any thoughts of marching into town and being allowed to sing her own songs in just the way she wanted, had always planned, she was in for a rude awakening.

Music making in Nashville is, first and foremost, a business just like any other. It has its own codes, institutions and ways of doing things which, with time, have become a particularly fine art. And just like any other business, the purse-holders and decision-makers are most interested in the bottom line. When it comes to making records, there tends to be a strict division of labour: the songwriters come up with the raw material, the studio musicians supply the finesse and the singer adds their own personal touch, their individual brand, fronting the whole operation and thereby keeping most of the kudos for him or herself. It's simple, it's efficient, it works. Everybody involved in the process understands it and it has made some people both very rich and very powerful. The downside is that the results can all too often sound like mere product: reliable, homogenous and bland. Still, that's the way it has always been, or at least since the late 1950s when country music first decided it wanted to clean up its hillbilly image and start appealing to a more urbane audience. Those hoping to buck the system usually find themselves banging their heads against a brick wall and, dismayed by the strict regimentation, drift off to more free-wheeling climes like California and Austin, Texas. Even for one with such a flexible career attitude as Shania, this hard reality was to prove rather less than a dream come true.

Having signed her up, Mercury-Nashville's answer to the question of what to do next with Shania was all too predictable. Still buoyant from the huge crossover success of Billy Ray Cyrus and his 'Achy Breaky Heart' (not forgetting the *Some Gave All* album either) during the summer of 1992, they fancied some more of the same. Shania was teamed up in the studio with Norro Wilson and another heavyweight producer with a good track record, Harold Shedd, the man who had not only helped turn country-rockers Alabama into a virtual hit machine but had also been responsible, as one of the label's senior vice-presidents, for obtaining Billy Ray Cyrus's lucrative signature as well. Plainly the expectation was that with this kind of experience behind the control desk, it would simply be a matter of sitting back and waiting for the hits to start piling up. Everybody is still waiting.

Released in the spring of 1993, Shania's self-titled debut album was a disappointment rather than a real artistic or commercial disaster. Even the critics, country music specialists or otherwise, were unable to summon up much enthusiasm one way

Below Guess what? This isn't Billy Ray Cyrus.

or the other. Although the record has long since been certified platinum, initial US sales totalled a modest 100,000: not a figure to be sneezed at, but not one likely to recoup the initial outlay or sustain too many thoughts of a lengthy career either. Nor were the reasons that hard to fathom, even at the time: the ten songs were a fairly stale bunch, while the production was the standard professional job, not a whole lot different from the dozens of other albums that slink through the Nashville factory gates each year. There's no sparkle or shine, just the enervating feeling that you are being led by the nose to places you have already been hundreds of times before on the likes of 'Crime Of The Century', 'Forget Me' and 'When He Leaves You'. Predictably, Shania gives it her best shot – she hadn't crawled on her hands and knees all this way for nothing, had she? – without ever suggesting she is in the same vocal league as Wynonna Judd or Reba McEntire, with their ability to get right under the skin of the most perfunctory lyric and rattle windows at 40 paces. With the benefit of hindsight, Shania's own assessment of the album is wonderfully telling: 'I don't hate the album, but I'm better singing songs I write.'

In the event, only one of Shania's tunes ('God Ain't Gonna Getcha For That', co-written with Kent Robbins) made it onto the final disc. For somebody who prided herself on her song-writing, it was a bitter pill to swallow. In particular, she was finding it hard adapting to Nashville's committee-like ways of drumming up hits. 'I was pushed into these three-hour writing sessions and I didn't understand any of it. People write like they're going to lunch together,' she has noted ruefully. Her own preferred method of wandering off into the forest for a couple of days and waiting for the inspiration to suddenly seize her, though, was patently no longer an option. Besides, Mercury wanted a singer, a star. In a town where competent tunesmiths are ten a penny, they rightly weren't interested in feather-bedding Shania's lingering creative aspirations when any fool could see that her best chance of making it would most likely come by concentrating on her sassy image and glowing looks. That, anyway, was the plan; and, in a strangely roundabout way, it worked.

With the bouncy 'What Made You Say That?', by some distance the album's most appealing track, being pitched as the lead single, Shania was shipped off to Miami for the promotional video shoot. What emerged might have been inordinately tame by prevailing rock, pop or rap standards, but it was deemed hot stuff in country music's more conservative circles. In truth, the thing didn't look like a country-music video at all. Not only was it set on a beach, it also had Shania cavorting around this sculpted,

shirtless male torso with a certain glint in her eye and her bellybutton showing for all the world to see. 'I didn't realise at first that the way I saw myself or wanted to be seen visually wasn't really going to be accepted. It allowed me to be myself, but nearly got me booted out of town too,' she told me backstage at her Toronto gig in August 1998. It did the trick, though. People even picked up on it in Hollywood and over in Europe, way beyond country music's core constituency. Unfortunately, the sight of all that ripe flesh did nothing at all for the record, which stalled unceremoniously at 55 in Billboard's country chart; a potentially lethal blow for any new artist where a hit single is as good as mandatory to help set an album's sales rolling.

Yet if Mercury were starting to have a few concerns about their investment they certainly weren't letting on. In fact, money appeared to be no object at all. For the first album's striking sleeve, Shania was even sent back to her own neck of the woods in northern Ontario. There, posed against the icy-blue tundra backdrop and swaddled in buckskin and fur, she stared out from behind a fire, with only a particularly handsome specimen of wolf for company. (Animal lovers may feel better for knowing the beast was a tame one called Cane who had been brought all the way over from

Far left The disappointment of her first album long forgotten, Shania on stage in Syracuse, New York, June 1999.

Vancouver for the privilege.) Anyone looking for a message in the record's design might happily conclude that the Shania pictured was not to be readily mistaken for just one of the pack. In reality, of course, that's precisely what she now was: an attractively moulded product with few distinguishing features.

In another effort to get her name across and start building a fan base, Shania was despatched on a 16-date promotional tour with fellow freshman labelmates, Toby Keith and John Brannen. Fighting every night for her share of attention with two equally eager-to-please newcomers was no picnic. She emerged from the experience with her reputation intact rather than enhanced, unlike Keith, who scored heavily with the chart-topping 'Should've Been A Cowboy'. Finding herself increasingly caught up in a machine with somebody else's hand on the controls, self-doubt began to surface. Was she really cut out for this kind of life? If all she was ever going to do was cover other people's songs, why hadn't she just stayed in Deerhurst, earned herself a decent living and been nearer to her family too? Having taken such a gigantic step towards achieving her lifetime's ambitions, Shania should have been in clover. Instead, she was beginning to feel more and more isolated. 'I guess I better not complain about being lonely,' she remarked at the time.

Success for the second single, 'Dance With The One That Brought You', looked to be crucial. Certainly the portents appeared favourable when, out of the blue, Hollywood hard guy Sean Penn, a man not generally known for his predilection for stetsons and rhinestone suits, had rung Mary Bailey and expressed an interest in directing Shania's next video. He had seen the previous one, he said, and been much impressed by all that frolicking. Filming duly took place during May 1993 with veteran movie actor, Charles Durning, taking one of the roles. It could have marked the beginning of a beautiful relationship between Nashville and Hollywood. Instead, for all the effort and expense, the single again

Top Beefy and bearded Toby Keith, an early touring partner.

Above Tough guy Sean Penn: some might say an unusual choice for directing one of Shania's videos. Seen here with his one-time wife, Madonna.

Far right Unperturbed by big-collar scare, Shania sings bravely on.

failed to find favour with the public at large, not even making the Top 40. Plainly something wasn't quite right, something that the poor performance of the album's third single, a gushy ballad called 'You Lay A Whole Lot Of Love On Me', underlined with a vengeance.

After one album, three singles, considerable amounts of green folding stuff and not a sniff of a hit, Shania and Mary's hard-earned vision was already beginning to fade away. 'I only realised later that I didn't have much time left at my label. If your first album doesn't work, do they really want to invest more money in you? They had barely scratched the surface of what I was capable of doing. I really thought it was all going to happen in stages, that I would have time to come into my own. I now know how quickly I would have been passed over,' Shania could afford to admit, looking back. What she didn't know at the time, however, was that fate had already intervened and come down firmly on her side. Thousands of miles away in England, somebody she had never even heard of had also grabbed a good eyeful of the video for 'What Made You Say That?' and was sufficiently intrigued to want to find out more. His name was 'Mutt' Lange and, putting it mildly, he knew all about hit records. He also reckoned he could help.

Mutt

Essentially, record producers come in two kinds. Most are quite content to take up a responsive, enabling, sometimes even passive role in the process of making a shiny little platter. In between the twiddling of knobs and endless cups of coffee, they flatter, coax, cajole and offer advice to their artists. If that doesn't work out, they simply get out the big stick, wave it around, shout and do precisely what they had in mind to do in the first place. After all, it's about getting a job done, of bringing a project home on time within an agreed budget — the same as anything else in this big, grown-up world.

It's how they do things in Nashville, for sure. It's a business after all. Time is money. You can be creative up to a point, but you can't afford to mess around, can you?

And then there's another sort, just an elite handful, maybe, for whom the studio is like their own personal playground, where the performers (themselves included, sometimes) are there to be used as just another instrument or piece of machinery. These are the creators, the control freaks, the ones with the big vision. They're always obsessive in their attention to detail, not caring how long something takes or what it costs just as long as it ends up sounding right. And, of course, only they will know when that precise moment arrives. They're people like Todd Rundgren, Phil Spector with his 'Wall Of Sound', the Italian synthesiser maestro Giorgio Moroder, Boston's tortoise-paced Tom Scholz (eight years to make his last

Far right Thank you, Mr Paparazzo. An incredibly rare picture of Shania and husband Mutt Lange together on their way to a performance of *Swan Lake* at London's Dominion Theatre in February 2000.

Above Paris, December 1998 at the Amnesty International Gala with an all-star cast including Bruce Springsteen, Radiohead and the Dalai Lama. Shania looking good in leather, riding that invisible bucking bronco. Hard to fathom what Mutt sees in her, isn't it?

album? Is that all?) and Kraftwerk's very odd couple, Ralf Hutter and Florian Schneider, who busy themselves every day in their own Klingklang studios yet still haven't quite got around to releasing anything new since 1986. The word 'genius' is sometimes applied in these circumstances, occasionally prefixed by another one: 'mad'.

There's another, though probably rather less familiar, name that needs to be added to that list, too. It's unfamiliar because that's precisely the way he likes it. Def Leppard's Joe Elliott calls him the greatest producer on earth and he has been responsible for some of the biggest-selling rock records ever made. His name is Robert John Lange, or 'Mutt', as he has been called since his schooldays. And the moment this lanky, intensely private and mysterious figure kind of shuffled sideways into Shania's life, things started to

happen for the better for them both. In fact, if you didn't know any better or weren't brought up to believe in fairytales, their rather unlikely coming together might sound like a work of pure fiction because it really is almost too good to be true.

Mutt Lange was born somewhere in South Africa in 1949, or possibly 1951. Nobody except Mutt seems to know, and he's not telling because he never speaks to the press – ever. Personal details are not so much sketchy, more missing. He is rumoured to have once been a singer himself, and even though he has been photographed about as frequently as the Loch Ness monster, he is said to be tall, blond and kind of ruggedly handsome in a shaggy sort of way. If he is trying to hide anything in his past, nobody has the faintest idea what that might actually be. It therefore seems fairly safe to assume that he is just one of those people who wants to be left alone. That's his privilege, after all.

By the mid-1970s, though, having relocated to London, Mutt's moniker was increasingly beginning to crop up among the production credits for long-gone and not-much-missed British bands such as City Boy, Supercharge and The Motors. This being the era of pub-rock and punk too, he was also keeping himself more than busy with XTC and the excellent jangly power

pop of The Records, as well as the white soul/Bruce Springsteen surrogate Graham Parker and Ireland's very lively Boomtown Rats, who were actually considered pretty nifty for a time in England back then; well, they had a few hits anyway. But his reputation really came to be made in 1979 when he linked up with Australia's generous gift to heavy metal, AC/DC, to helm their breakthrough album *Highway To Hell*, together with the band's subsequent worldwide successes *Back In Black* (10 million US units shifted), *For Those About To Rock (We Salute You)* and *Who Made Who*.

Above Shania fighting her way through a wind tunnel during her ever-expanding world tour. Glen Helen Blockbuster Pavilion, May 1999.

Above Def Leppard's Joe Elliott and Phil Collen rocking out. Pre-Shania, they were Mutt's most successful production job.

Far right Shania going home with another armful, this time from 1998's Billboard Music Awards.

Whatever exactly was involved in this production lark, Mutt had obviously cracked it. Not only that, he could write a bit too, as evidenced by a C.V. that includes hits like 'Do You Believe In Love?' for Huey Lewis And The News, '(Everything I Do) I Do It For You' with Bryan Adams and a whole handful for the disco-lite Billy Ocean, such as 'When The Going Gets Tough, The Tough Get Going'. Among his many attributes, Mutt possesses a very highly developed pop ear, which he can turn in just about any direction. And when you're in the business of trying to make hit records, that's a very rare and precious commodity indeed.

The following decade he continued to refine his skills in the studio and cement his reputation for perfectionism, a combination that would include Foreigner's *Foreigner 4* album (10 weeks at the top of the US album charts) and The Cars' *Heartbeat City*, a record that would yield five US Top 40 singles, including the unforgettable 'Drive'. The results were truly spectacular even if Mutt's working practices were not always appreciated by those subjected to them. 'He just made us do it over and over again,' recalls XTC's Andy Partridge. The Cars' Ric Ocasek is a touch more specific: 'Mutt used to say, "Nobody ever listens to the lyrics anyway, so who gives a shit?" I like Mutt but he has firm beliefs about things like that.' Besides, as Bryan Adams puts it, 'Let's be honest, Mutt could work with my mom and have hit records.' Fortunately, or not (we'll never know), Mrs Adams was never pressed into service to test this particular theory. What should be clear from all of this, however, is that when it comes to logging up multi-million sellers, Mutt Lange has had precious few equals over the last two decades. And as if all that wasn't enough, there was Def Leppard too.

Often credited as being The Sixth Leppard, so closely is he associated with their success, Mutt took these young, raw northern Englishmen and turned them into purest gold. Their first album together, *High 'n' Dry*, in 1981 pretty much established the blueprint for what was to follow without managing to set the charts alight. Their next, though, 1983's *Pyromania* (appropriately enough) did; changing the shape and sound of heavy rock in one fell swoop. Here were not just bone-crushing guitar riffs of inestimable tonnage but also tunes with great, sculpted choruses too, layers and layers of them, piled high and proud, which proved to be all but irresistible to both heavy-rock and pop fans alike. In the charts it was kept off the top spot only by Michael Jackson's *Thriller* and it would notch up a cool six million sales during the year. But even that was nothing compared with the next highly collaborative effort, 1987's triumphant *Hysteria*; a project that, at times, looked almost doomed.

Things got off to the worst possible start when Leppard's drummer, Rick Allen, mislaid his left arm in a car smash on New Year's Eve, 1984. Rather than giving up there and then, however, Allen eventually battled back with the aid of a purpose-built kit that would allow him to activate rolls and fills with his feet. Mutt, too, was having some problems of his own. He had initially declined to sit once again in the producer's chair due to mental and physical exhaustion. Yet with the sessions apparently floundering badly in his absence, he was talked back into overseeing matters in July 1985. Still, there was another hitch to come, as Mutt himself was involved in a head-on automobile accident in November 1986 while on his way to the studios in Dublin, Ireland, where recordings were taking place. That put him out of action for three weeks. It might have been much, much worse.

Was *Hysteria* really worth all the time, effort, money (about $1.5 million, they reckon) and pain spent on making it? Once more, the results said

Yes. It would eventually sell more than 17 million copies and it spawned a total of seven US Top 100 singles, putting it in a truly exalted league alongside efforts by Bruce Springsteen and, individually, Michael and Janet Jackson. And, of course, Mutt was a heck of a lot more than just the producer; he was also credited as co-writer and backing vocalist. By anyone's standards, he was at the top of his profession. He was the studio magician who made things happen, who virtually guaranteed success. He was, as Def Leppard's Phil Collen put it, 'the most easy-going dictator you'll ever meet'.

To those who like to think that rock 'n' roll, whatever its hue, is all to do with feel and instinct, Mutt remains anathema. His methods of building a single track up slowly, meticulously, layer by layer, line by line, phrase by phrase and not moving on until it finally meets with his complete approval – an hour, a day, a week, whatever it takes – removes any sense of randomness from the process. Yet the sheer attention to detail of everything bearing his imprint continues to stagger, even if ultimately the artistry and creativity that is being applauded tends to be as much his as the performer's. Fellow studio obsessive Jim Steinman sums him up neatly: 'Mutt's just like Frankenstein. He pieces little bits of

skin together.' Yet the results always sound fantastic on the radio or the stereo. Like any good painting or a photograph, there's always something new to discover; something you never quite noticed before, even though you may have looked at it a hundred times. Sure, it's a product, but it can still be a work of art too.

During the 1990s, Mutt began to take his foot off the pedal a touch, at least as to the number of projects he was undertaking. Still as meticulous as ever, though, his work on Bryan Adams' *Waking Up The Neighbours* (1991) almost predictably overran, this time to the extent that he was unable to take up full production duties on Def Leppard's *Adrenalize*. (He was still credited as co-producer, but apparently did most of it by relaying directions to Joe Elliott over the phone.) Equally predictable was the Canadian rocker's album's success and one song in particular, '(Everything I Do) I Do It For You'; a cumbersome title, yet another worldwide smash and one that would not only top the US and Canadian charts, but also be the UK's longest-ever-running Number One (sixteen weeks). Mutt produced it and co-wrote it. It remains his biggest success to date. Then, out of the blue, something different caught his eye. Or, rather, somebody.

Spring 1993, London: Mutt is, as ever,

beavering away in the studio. In one corner the TV is on. Country Music Television Europe is playing; it often is. It turns out that despite his heavy-metal credentials Mutt is a bit of a sucker for fiddles and steel guitars. On comes this video of a very fit-looking young woman cavorting about in the surf with a chap whose shirt is no longer where it was designed to be. This is hardly traditional country-music fare, he notices. Mutt, being mere flesh and blood and, as Tammy Wynette once so eloquently put it, 'just a man', decides that he likes what he sees: nice teeth, for instance. But there's more to it than that. Sure, the voice is good and strong as well. Yet he recognises there's an extra sparkle about this person up on the screen, maybe even a hunger and an ambition. He thinks he could do something for this woman with the unusual name. S-H-A-N-I-A: how exactly do you pronounce that? And again? She deserves some better material, for a start. He thinks he's the man for the job. Resolving to find out more, he tries to make some sort of initial contact.

Having tracked down Shania's record company – no great task for a man of his calibre, however reticent – he calls the number. They in turn pass him onto Shania's manager, Mary Bailey. He speaks to Mary, explains who he is and that his intentions are entirely honourable. She's

never heard of him. Why should she? He might be a hot-shot, multi-million dollar record producer but he's got a public image that could happily slip under a closed door. Besides, what sort of name is Mutt? And that accent, too? Where did he get that from? Mary does what she normally does on these occasions when somebody wants to get a little closer to Shania but doesn't sound exactly dangerous: she takes the caller's details and sends out a signed photograph of her client. Well, it's better than a kick on the shins. Good picture, actually. Definitely an improvement on Def Leppard's Joe Elliott.

Above Bryan Adams, another one of Mutt's grateful client bank. Everything he does he does for us, Bryan once told the world.

You Win My Love

'It was definitely a force that brought us together. Something drove him and I'm not sure even he knew what it was,' is how Shania has tried to describe how Mutt came into her life. Indeed, had he fallen out of the sky and landed in a heap at her feet she could hardly have been more amazed at how things turned out. Let's face it, this kind of thing only happens in the movies; and even then only when it's starring Tom Hanks and Meg Ryan.

Despite being fobbed off a few times, Mutt manfully persisted in his telephonic pursuit of the woman with the midriff. Eventually he was rewarded for his perseverance by getting to speak to her in person. 'I had no idea he was a world-famous record producer. I didn't read the back of pop and rock albums, which was good because I wasn't intimidated by him. Otherwise, I don't think I would have been able to express myself creatively without any

inhibitions,' she has claimed. Though thousands of miles apart, a friendship quickly developed between the two, with music as their shared love, their obsession. Certainly something must have clicked.

He said he really liked her voice and asked her whether she wrote her own songs. She said she did, also telling him how she was getting frustrated at not getting the chance to sing them there in Nashville. Being a bit of a gent, he made the

'It was definitely a force that brought us together. Something drove him and I'm not sure even he knew what it was.'

appropriate soothing noises and asked her to sing him one of them over the phone. Who could resist such solicitous wooing? Certainly not one as driven as Shania. She rested the receiver on her pillow (it was an intimate moment, after all), and sang him the chorus of 'Home Ain't Where The Heart Is (Anymore)', the swooningly sad ballad that would open the *The Woman In Me* album. Mutt responded in kind with something of his own; one called 'Said I Loved You But I Lied' which was about to be a hit for the capaciously lunged Michael Bolton. Soon they were regularly swapping ideas and singing half-finished songs to one another down the wires.

At that precise moment in her life, this long-distance relationship was precisely the sustenance Shania needed. Here, after all, was this seriously big record producer taking quality time out to offer words of advice and encouragement when nobody else seemed bothered. She was being treated as a professional equal. She was flattered. So what if they had never met? She wasn't looking for romance. What's more, there was an obvious empathy between the pair of them. Still, in her mind's eye, Shania couldn't help trying to picture the face at the other end of the line. 'I always thought he'd look like some fat old roadie with long, grey hair tied in a straggly ponytail,' was the best she could come up with. Mutt, of course, knew exactly who he was talking to. And it was definitely no sack of potatoes.

After a few weeks of running up pocket-emptying transatlantic phone bills, the two finally met face to face for the first time in June 1993. The venue was Nashville's Tennessee State Fairgrounds; the occasion the annual Fan Fair shindig. Ever since 1972, this has been a unique attraction in the music-business calendar. While for outsiders, the week-long event might easily resemble purgatory right here on earth, for thousands of dyed-in-the-wool country-music afficionados it's the one immovable fixture in the diary; an

unmissable opportunity to mingle with like-minded souls, snaffle up armfuls of souvenirs, catch a few live showcases, pig out and, for a couple of precious seconds, get real close to your musical idols.

Under a baking-hot sun, fans queue for hour after hour to claim their autographs of all the stars in the Nashville firmament; the bigger the name, the longer the wait. So it goes. Garth Brooks, Vince Gill, Reba McEntire, they all come and sit in their customised booths, doing their duty. Not to attend would be seen as the height of bad manners. For somebody at the bottom of the pile like Shania, however, being there is all but compulsory. The reasoning is simple: it's all about touching base. Besides, maybe a few more people will go out and buy your record when they've got a signed photo at

home. With the first album making only ripples not waves, she definitely had her work cut out trying to make an impression. One visitor to her booth she didn't need to impress, of course, was Mutt. They greeted one another like old friends. In fact, she was pleasantly surprised by her phone buddy. 'In walked this neat-looking, tall, thin guy with long, curly blond hair and blue eyes,' she recalls.

If there was a mutual attraction right from that first meeting, initially the relationship was purely, platonically business only. Yet though Mutt quickly returned to Europe and Shania continued trying to flog her first album, the phone lines between the two remained as busy as ever. Better still, they had already agreed they would try working together in the near future. For Mutt there

Above Accepting a small floral tribute from an admirer. Shame about the wrapping paper.

would be the opportunity to broaden his musical palette; for Shania there was now suddenly the irresistible appeal of having one of the most successful names in rock offering to assist her in wresting control of her own career. Indeed, not only would he place her on a pedestal, he would actually build it and help finance it too. Talk about a ship coming in. This was an ocean liner. Full steam ahead.

In the autumn of 1993 Mutt invited Shania over to London for a working holiday around Europe. He suggested she took Concorde. She had never heard of it, but what can a girl do? They travelled around France, Spain and Italy together, fashioning songs and getting closer and closer. The inevitable happened. As she tried explaining to *Rolling Stone*, '… we pretty much wrote almost all of the album [*The Woman In Me*] before we even revealed our feelings to each other, which wasn't long. It was kind of exciting, actually. It's very funny because I've always been that way. I've never, ever, ever let a guy know the way I felt about him until I know, because I'm just never a fool for that. I don't know whether I'm just really old-fashioned that way or what. But I just always felt there's no point making a fool of yourself, you know. Just feel it out for a little while. I just feel I've never been rushed about those things, I

guess is what I'm saying. Just one day we hugged each other. But it was such a different kind of hug, and that was actually when we knew, right there. So it wasn't a kiss. So it wasn't like a very sexual or passionate moment. It was a very sweet, honest moment.'

In Paris, never a bad place for getting down on one knee, Mutt whipped out a big diamond ring and asked for Shania's hand in marriage. 'I knew it was coming because he had invited my sisters along,' she has said. And so, less than six months after first setting eyes on one another, here she was saying yes. With the clocks barely having a chance to pause for breath, they wed on 28 December 1993 back at Deerhurst, with just a few friends and relatives present. In the one photo celebrating the occasion since given to the press, Mutt is distinctly absent. With his 'X' always placed firmly in the no-publicity box, that was the way he wanted it. 'It's embarrassing to him. It's corny to him and I totally understand it,' is Shania's avowed attitude to her spouse's pathological shunning of the limelight. Others, however, have since used Mutt's 'non-presence' to raise doubts about the foundations of such a high-profile relationship where the two parties are never seen in public together, not even in their wedding snaps. Not that there's anything to go on, mind. 'He's a very

'He's a very
humble guy and
basically doesn't
want to be a
star. He just
wants to be a
person who
makes music.'

Left Looking a tad pensive,
don't you think? Never
mind, world domination is
just around the corner.

humble guy and basically doesn't want to be a star. He just wants to be a person who makes music,' she told *Country Weekly* in 1996. Nothing has changed since.

Given the modest success of her first album, Shania was in no position at all to call the shots when it came to making her second; until Mutt came on the scene, that is. 'I was saved. I was going to be creative again,' she exclaimed. Not only did her new husband believe in her totally – in his mind she was a diamond simply waiting to be polished – but he was also prepared to back that judgement with his own hard cash. Prior to entering Nashville's Sound Stage studio at the beginning of 1994, a highly unusual deal was struck with Mercury whereby, in return for complete artistic control, Mutt would fund the recording largely out of his own deep pockets. 'That's a beautiful relationship to have with a creative person,' label chief Luke Lewis is quoted as saying, presumably with a big grin. He wasn't kidding. Taking the best part of a year to put together and costing a reputed half-million dollars (the most expensive album in Nashville's history by miles), the new Shania-Mutt team proceeded to break every rule in the Music City book when it came to *The Woman In Me*. Things haven't been the same since.

For a start, there was not the usual beauty

parade when it came to picking the songs; it was a complete in-house job. Ten of the album's dozen tracks are joint Twain/Lange compositions while the remaining two, 'You Win My Love' and 'Leaving Is The Only Way Out', are respectively credited to Mutt and Shania on their own. The slant of the lyrics was distinctly different too; dare one say, rather more in keeping with how things were in the late twentieth century. Whereas

Above Accepting her Blockbuster Award and doing the Charleston at the same time poses no problems at all for Shania.

before she was being asked to play the traditional role of the infinitely faithful wife/mother, seemingly forever awaiting the return of her errant male, now, given a free hand, she could be the young woman she really was: in her prime, able to give as good as she gets, fully capable of making her own life choices (including saying no) thank you very much, yet sometimes vulnerable too. As for the sonic shape of the record, it naturally possesses all the hallmarks of a typical labour-intensive Mutt Lange production: full of finely tweaked hooks with a big, thick, textured sound that jumps out of the speakers just like those Def Leppard albums. Sure, the steel guitars and fiddles are still there, but there's a snap, a fizzle, a real poke to it, not forgetting quirky little touches like the way '(If You're Not In It For Love) I'm Outta Here!' closes with a huffy sigh, high heels clicking across the room and a slamming door. It's fun, it's lively, it's entertaining, and it's an awful long way from Hank Williams, God rest his soul.

Together, just as they had planned, Shania and Mutt had broken the mould. They knew they had done a great job. Shania figured that given a good following wind and some proper promotion, the album might go triple platinum. There was no shortage of doubting Thomases out there, though, and predictably the album went down like a lead balloon in conservative Nashville right from the moment it was released in January 1995. Who, after all, did this woman, this outsider, think she was, with her big ideas and her rock-producer husband turning up and turning things upside down? Had she no respect? Responding to accusations that she was too 'pop' for country, Shania merely shrugged and pointed out that pop now went all the way from Snoop Doggy Dogg to Celine Dion; the lines had long since blurred and she was simply being herself. 'We're just all people who make music for the purpose of pleasing as many people as we can. That's the idea,' she told the *Toronto Sun*.

Typical of the uphill struggle that Shania initially faced was the refusal of CMTV's selection committee to place the video for the first single, 'Whose Bed Have Your Boots Been Under?' on heavy rotation because it was considered 'too sexy'. Of course, there's a fair bit of waggling, shimmying and pouting on view, not to mention Shania's enthusiastic teasing of some frankly terrified-looking male diners, but nothing that most of us won't have seen before, ooh, about a million times; just better packaged, maybe. Anyway, as the record started taking off (eventually peaking at number 11, her best yet), the station

was forced to double-back and put it higher up the schedules. Contrary to the wishes of a few, the many had spoken. Indeed, the public were beginning to develop quite a taste for the Canadian and her ways.

The breakthrough finally arrived with the next single, 'Any Man Of Mine'. Inevitably there was another bellybutton-revealing video which, just like its predecessor had been, was directed by the late John Derek, the Svengali-like husband of Bo – yes, the 'perfect-bodied' *Ten* of movie infamy. The two of them had been brought in as the songstress's image consultants, which probably says plenty. (Derek also took responsibility for the *The Woman In Me*

Above John and Bo Derek, the Mr and Mrs team behind Shania's raunchy image refit.

Far left Shania digitally celebrates one million Canadian sales of *The Woman In Me*.

Above Under clear blue skies, definitely the healthy
outdoors look, featuring the infamous bared midriff that sent
Nashville tongues wagging.

Far right If you've got it, flaunt it! Sporty and relaxed at
London's Party In The Park, July 1999.

album cover, featuring a Shania who, oddly, appears to have just spent a spectacularly rough night in a hedge.) This time, though, in keeping with the track's clappy hoe-down brief and angled straight at the line-dance market, Shania acts like she's the world's bounciest, healthiest farm girl as she delivers her shopping list of wants for guys who might fancy their chances. 'He's gotta be a heartbeatin' fine treatin'/Breathtakin' earthquakin' kind,' she throatily chirrups. The outcome was a Number One country single in July 1995. When she paid a return visit to Fan Fair during that same month, this time it was as the hottest up-and-coming country star in town, even without Nashville's formal blessing. Now for the rest of the planet, then.

In quick succession a touring band was put together for promotional duties, including a trip to the UK to play three showcases for the usual array of media and record-company types. There was also a video shoot in Egypt for the album's gorgeous title track which would memorably show the diaphanously clad Shania suggestively fondling some ancient columns ('I need you baby', indeed). Then it was back to California for some much needed national TV exposure courtesy of an appearance on the *Tonight* show, with other slots being quickly inked in.

By now the album was steadily building a momentum beyond the usual country baseline. As night follows day, so the next step would have normally been a six-month slog around North America, touring the album, supporting a bigger-named Nashville act; Wynonna Judd was mentioned. Instead, Shania stunned everybody (including her own record company) by announcing she would not be going on the road at all. The time wasn't right, she said. 'I came to the conclusion that there was no way I was gonna be able to compete show-wise with Reba, Wynonna, etc., and if I can't compete with them, then I'm not gonna make an impression,' was her explanation to the *Journal Of Country Music*. To her detractors, the decision simply proved she was just a video puppet, a studio creation who – whisper it softly – couldn't really sing. Obviously those two decades spent at the sharp end paying her dues didn't count.

Yet rather than sitting at home with her feet up, Shania instead concentrated on promoting herself and her album in any way she possibly could: prestigious TV like *Late Night With Letterman*, selected press interviews, special 'fan days', album signings, you name it, she'd be there. Naturally, each time she looked fabulous, like the proverbial million dollars. Certainly no Nashville star had ever been as image-conscious; she was a true product of the MTV generation and it showed. The cameras loved her. For the video for '(If You're Not In It For Love) I'm Outta Here!' she took a reputed five hours to be squeezed into her skintight pants. Everything had to be just so. Still, it was definitely paying off. By the beginning of November 1995 her second album had notched up over three million sales. Later in the month she would sing for the Clintons at a gala event in Washington and ride through New York on a giant turkey float at the annual Thanksgiving Day parade. More than a mere celebrity, she was fast becoming a Stateside phenomenon. And amazingly, things were only just starting.

Moving Forward

By late 1995 it was clear that Shania's second album had acquired a life and momentum all of its own; it just kept on selling, week after week, month after month. Rather than letting nature take its course, the decision to continuously 'work' *The Woman In Me* through high-profile promotion and a steady drip-feed of singles and videos (an incredible eight of the record's dozen tracks would be released in a radio-friendly format) was paying off better than anybody could have possibly imagined.

Just like any other business, the music industry likes to celebrate its winners and, plainly, such success could not be ignored for long. The first official recognition of Shania's achievements came when the Canadian Country Music Association lavished seven nominations upon her at their annual awards. What's more, she walked off with the prize in five categories, including three of the big ones: Female Vocalist Of The Year, Album Of The Year and Single Of The Year for 'Any Man Of Mine'. Tellingly, though, she was not so fortunate when it came to the much more prestigious US Country Music Association awards. Despite being nominated for Video Of The Year, Single Of The Year and the Horizon Award for 'creative growth', she found herself being overlooked by Nashville. It wouldn't be for the last time.

Somebody who would no longer be sharing in Shania's remarkable rise to fame,

however, was Mary Bailey. Shortly after a live performance at the Billboard Awards Show held at the New York Coliseum in December, Mary was informed that her services were no longer required. It was a bitter blow for one who had been a virtual mother figure to the singer for the best part of a decade and who had done as much as anybody to help put her where she was today. Shania spoke briefly of not wanting to get 'caught in a comfort zone' and 'needing to move forward'. Mary said very little at all, accepting her fate with grace and dignity, probably aware that as her charge's horizons continued to grow bigger and bigger, a more demonstrative style of management than she could offer would be required. Eventually, Jon Landau, Bruce Springsteen's long-standing manager, got the job, as good an indication as any as to where Shania now saw herself heading.

A new year brought more of the same. In January 1996 Shania found herself being garlanded at the American Music Awards as Favorite New Country Artist, chatting on TV with Oprah Winfrey and opening a new sports arena in Vancouver. There were also another batch of her special 'fan days' in Minneapolis, Dallas, Toronto and Calgary; her very own Fan Fairs, if you like. By February, a whole twelve months after its release, sales for the album had leapt to five

Above The Juno award, a handsome addition to any bathroom cabinet.

Left Another useful household implement for the collection, this time picked up at the American Music Awards.

Far left Take a deep breath. If this is Monday, it must be the Billboard Awards. Or was that last week?

million and showed no sign of faltering. In March, at the Juno Awards (Canada's equivalent of the Grammys), she walked away with Country Female Vocalist Of The Year and Entertainer Of The Year, despite being directly pitted against Alanis Morissette, whose *Jagged Little Pill* album had also proved to be one of the runaway hits of the 1990s.

All seemed to be going swimmingly, until Shania found herself under personal attack from a most unexpected quarter. On 5 April, the *Timmins Daily Press* published an article headed 'Shania Twain's "other" family criticises red-hot singer'. The thrust of the

'I guess you know you've made a certain level when you make the tabloids.'

Far right Come to mama. Shania gets confused and practices her resuscitation techniques on an inanimate object at the 38th Annual Grammy Awards.

piece was that she had not only chosen to ignore her true biological father, Clarence Edwards, and his family, but that she had also overplayed her Native Indian blood when, in fact, she didn't have any at all. It all got a bit heated for a while, with Shania threatening legal action against the paper and swiftly issuing her own press statement, which read, in part: 'Although I was briefly introduced to Clarence a couple of times in my teen years, I never knew him growing up. My mother did not deprive us of knowledge of his existence. She let us know where he lived, what he did for a living, a little about his family background and that there was some Indian heritage in his family. That's what I was raised to believe and know from her to be true. I never deliberately avoided contact with the Edwards family, but my father Jerry's parents loved us as though we were their very own grandchildren and we were equally accepted by his other relatives.'

Interestingly, Clarence refused to talk directly to the press, a move for which he must be given credit. As for the story itself, perhaps it's best to consider it a piece of overenthusiastic journalism from a couple of reporters who had managed to track the man down to a bare scratch on the map called Chapleau in Ontario, hoping to find some grime behind the golden-girl image. From a distance, the episode now has all the appearance of a storm in a teacup. Do we really care if Shania has embellished her myth a touch or two? Whose business is her past other than her own? Anyway, who doesn't have a few skeletons of their own rattling around the closet? Unfortunately, worse was quickly to follow when her two half-brothers, Mark and Darryl, were arrested for trying to break into a car dealership in Huntsville, with Mark being handed down a six-month jail sentence. Again the media had a field day, raking over the past. 'I guess you know you've made a certain level when you make the tabloids,' she commented ruefully. Obviously, having such a successful big sister brings its own share of problems, not to mention unwanted publicity.

Back at the Tennessee State Fairgrounds in June for Fan Fair 1996, Shania was at least temporarily able to put those incidents behind her and concentrate on being herself again. Certainly, the public had shown that they didn't give two hoots about any smudgy side issues. By now, *The Woman In Me* had gone seven-times platinum, making it the biggest-selling album by a female in country-music history; suddenly she was right up there knocking on Garth Brooks' door. There was plenty to celebrate, which she duly did with a sparkling five-song set – 'Any Man Of Mine', 'Home Ain't Where The Heart Is (Anymore)', 'You Win My Love', 'No One Needs To Know', '(If You're Not In It For Love) I'm Outta Here!' – performed before an adoring 20,000-strong crowd at the Mercury-Nashville show. It was her only live performance with a full band during the whole year and, ever the consummate professional, not even a failed monitor could put her off. She had suffered far greater hardships in her time than a little earpiece not working, hadn't she?

Another first occurred on 15 August, when Shania returned to Timmins to be greeted by the mayor and handed the keys to the town. Despite slashing rain, thousands turned out to witness the

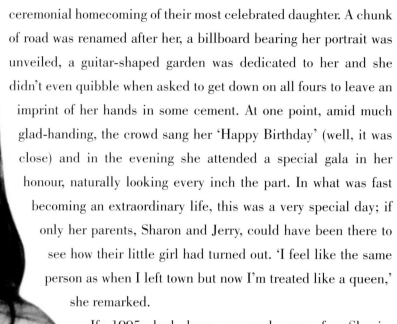

ceremonial homecoming of their most celebrated daughter. A chunk of road was renamed after her, a billboard bearing her portrait was unveiled, a guitar-shaped garden was dedicated to her and she didn't even quibble when asked to get down on all fours to leave an imprint of her hands in some cement. At one point, amid much glad-handing, the crowd sang her 'Happy Birthday' (well, it was close) and in the evening she attended a special gala in her honour, naturally looking every inch the part. In what was fast becoming an extraordinary life, this was a very special day; if only her parents, Sharon and Jerry, could have been there to see how their little girl had turned out. 'I feel like the same person as when I left town but now I'm treated like a queen,' she remarked.

If 1995 had been a good year for Shania, commercially speaking, 1996 had knocked it into a cocked hat. *The Woman In Me* had become a huge hit in both the country and pop charts, a true crossover smash that would eventually place it in the truly exalted company of Carole King's *Tapestry* and just a handful of others. Only one thing was missing: some sort of recognition from Nashville. A perfect opportunity to rectify the situation again presented itself with October's annual Country Music Association awards; surely Shania wouldn't go away empty-handed once more, would she? But just as twelve months previously, she was nominated in three categories – Song Of The Year, Best Female Vocalist, Horizon Award – so again was she passed over, this time to Vince Gill, Patty Loveless and Bryan White respectively. By following their own agenda, Shania and Mutt had obviously upset more than a few people in town. 'I'm not one of their creations, so a lot of people there might be offended by that,' she explained to me a couple of years later. 'Because I don't co-write with their writers I'm not involved with the whole music community the way a lot of artists there are. I'm naturally very independent.' Luckily, she could now afford to be.

One of those who found Shania's snubbing all a bit too fishy was Reba McEntire, whose own crown the Canadian had now effectively usurped, yet who still found it appropriate to deliver a highly excitable broadside in her defence. 'I wish the whole business of country music would join forces and kick it in the butt again. And when we get a Shania Twain, let's nominate her for album of the year, for Pete's sake. This woman has sold 10 million copies. Who in the thunder else has done that? What else does she have to do? I think she's got showmanship, she's beautiful, she can sing. It's almost like everybody is jealous of her success and I don't like it,' she told David Zimmerman of *USA Today*.

Frankly, by this stage, Shania's popularity had grown to such proportions that she really didn't need Nashville's blessing. In a roundabout way, the slighting may have made her even more determined not to be pigeonholed or limited in the public imagination as just another country singer like McEntire and the rest. She had her own distinct vision of where she wanted to be: in

'I'm naturally very independent.'

Left Country diva Reba McEntire, one of Shania's most vocal Nashville supporters.

Far left Well, you can't please everybody. Empty-handed (again) at the Country Music Awards, Nashville, September 1997.

Shania, country music had always been more a means to an end than simply an end in itself. Sure, she may have worshipped at the feet of Dolly Parton as a youngster, but she had been equally besotted by the toasty tones of Karen Carpenter's once peerless balladry, fantasised about being one of Stevie Wonder's backing vocalists and had, lest we forget, spent a large portion of her life singing just about every known style in the late-twentieth-century pop catalogue. In her own book, she was simply a singer: the category was irrelevant.

Unfazed by the ghosts of the past, a place where others saw or heard only boundaries and restrictions, she and Mutt had instead sensed only freedom and possibilities, using country music as a springboard to take them wherever they pleased. Isn't that what pop, in its purest sense, is supposed to have been about ever since Elvis first curled his lip? What's more, they had been entirely vindicated by *The Woman In Me*'s success where it counts: in the shops – 17 million units sold around the world, and counting. Of course, not everybody liked what she was doing or stood for – many detractors are still waiting for her to fall flat on her face – yet together the pair had genuinely created something fresh while, more pertinently, also hitting home with the ordinary man and woman in the street. It was an extraordinary

the big entertainment pond, swimming and competing with the likes of Madonna, Mariah Carey and Whitney Houston, women who had similarly transcended their musical origins and earned the right to be judged strictly on their own terms. For feat from a virtual standing start. The only question was how could Shania ever hope to repeat it?

Come On Over was released in the States during the first week of November 1997. This time people were waiting for it, suitably warmed up by the album's lead single, 'Love Gets Me Every Time', a bouncy number about the often unexpected trajectory of Cupid's capricious arrow. Once again, a few country-music radio stations considered the track 'too rock' for their playlists, only to back down when the public made their own feelings known. As for the album, it shipped gold within a matter of weeks, debuting at number one in the country charts and two in the all-genre pop listings. Within three months it had achieved triple-platinum status.

Suspicions that Shania might be a one-trick pony were immediately laid to rest; she was obviously here for the duration. In fact, *Come On Over* turned out to be just like *The Woman In Me*, only more so; both bigger (16 tracks, all Twain/Lange compositions; nearly an hour's worth of music) and better, with all the stops being pulled out. Over the next two years it would also help establish her as an international star, one of the most instantly recognisable faces, voices and middle portions in the world; the UK, Holland, Australia, India and beyond all eventually succumbing to her charms.

As ever, the critics were divided as to what Shania had managed to achieve with the album. While *Billboard* was prepared to admit that '... Twain and Lange continue to test the limits of country music and sometimes go far beyond them. In a very real sense, this is the future of power pop merging with country. In the process, country's traditions are being reinvented and redefined', *Rolling Stone* was among the many that were just plain sneering. Try this for size: 'The first thing you notice about Shania Twain's *Come On Over*, once you get past the pretty pictures on the cover, is how the titles have way too many exclamation points: "Man! I Feel Like A

Above When you're smiling, the whole world smiles with you, they reckon. Shania gives it her best shot.

Far left Shania demonstrates the impracticalities of PVC in her own inimitable fashion.

'It always offends me when people take the liberty to knock you, because artistically you can't — there are no rights and wrongs …'

Woman!", "Whatever You Do! Don't!" So does the music. Almost every high-gloss song opens with a bubblegum glam-cheerleader shout ("C'mon, girls!" "Cool!" "Kick it!" "Owww!"), then blasts into radio-ready rapture with offhand vocal interjections – doot-doot-doot scatting, do-si-dos, rapping, sexy squeaks, sarcastic Alanis Morissette asides. Twain bombards you with plastic hooks as tight as her trousers; the only reliable concessions to country tradition are all the fast fiddle-breakdown interruptions, and even those usually sound closer to classical figures than to square dances.' And there was plenty more where that came from. Nor were the country or daily press necessarily any more forgiving. A reviewer for *Country Monthly* considered the album suitable only for the ears of a ten-year-old child while the *Toronto Star* found the whole experience 'contrived' and 'nauseating'.

For her part, Shania is old enough to know that criticism is all part of the job: the higher you raise your head above the parapet, the easier you are to hit. That doesn't stop it sometimes hurting, though. 'I do get offended. But I don't get offended at their [the critics'] analysis of the whole thing, but it always offends me when people take the liberty to knock you, because artistically you can't – there are no rights and wrongs … this isn't like a race, you know, this isn't like that guy crossed the finish line first so he's the best runner,' she told *Rolling Stone*. Besides, for every grouchy reviewer with a bee in his or her bonnet, there are tens of thousands of fans who will happily tell you that Shania is the best thing since the pop-up toaster or the microwave oven and a whole lot more fun than either.

With *Come On Over* doing sweet business in the shops, Shania once again got stuck right into promoting both it and herself all over again with the rigour of a well-oiled presidential campaign. While life-size cardboard cut-outs of her were despatched to hundreds of record stores, the real thing was busily pressing the flesh, making herself readily available on the TV chat-show circuit and hosting more of her special fan days. In Calgary, for instance, 20,000-plus people turned out to catch a glimpse of her and grab an autograph at a local shopping mall. The awards, too, kept on coming.

At the 1998 Junos in March, she picked up the prize for Country Female Vocalist Of The Year for the second year running, despite missing out to Sarah McLachlan in the categories for Best Album and Female Vocalist. It hardly mattered. The following month she was in New York, taking part in the glitzy *Divas Live!* benefit concert organised by VH–1 to help raise funding for music tuition in public schools. An enthusiastic supporter of children's charities, Shania found herself sharing the limelight with Mariah Carey, Aretha Franklin, Celine Dion and Gloria Estefan, a real stellar line-up.

One of the evening's undoubted highlights was a wonderfully relaxed version of 'You're Still The One'. If Shania was looking for a signature tune, a single song that would perhaps come to define her in popular memory, this swooning, double-Grammy-winning ballad of dedication suddenly seemed to fit the bill perfectly. 'I think it's just one of those songs that a lot of people relate to. It doesn't really matter what genre you particularly listen to. I think that there are a lot of people, of all ages

even, that have succeeded at love against all odds. It kind of champions successful love and relationships,' she explained. During the summer months of 1998 'You're Still The One' was increasingly everywhere, a welcome bonus as the Canadian bombshell launched her first headlining tour.

Above Definitely best bib and tucker for VH–1's *Divas Live!* concert, April 1998.

On Top Of The World

What was billed as Shania's first-ever world tour kicked off on May 29, 1998 with two nights at Sudbury Arena, Ontario. Over the next three months she and her nine-piece band would criss-cross their way around US and Canadian stadiums and amphi-theatres, from Vancouver, Portland and Anaheim on the west coast through Denver, Kansas City, St Louis and Detroit, to gigs in Washington, Boston and New York State on the eastern flank. That, however, was just the start. As *Come On Over* continued selling like the hottest of hot cakes, more and more dates kept on being added.

By early December, when the show reached Fargo, North Dakota, one million ticket sales had been reached. She eventually found herself on the road, on and off, for a full 18 months right up until November 1999, grossing an estimated $63 million along the way. The risk she had taken by not touring until she was absolutely ready, a fully formed star in the popular imagina-tion, had proved to be 100 per cent justified. People were desperate to catch her in the flesh, to see for themselves what she was (or wasn't) wearing and whether she could possibly live up to the formidable buzz that had been built up around her on disc, on TV, on radio and in the press for the past three years. The simple answer was yes, she could.

The two-hour show was a huge, eye-popping spectacle with nothing left to chance. Four gigantic video screens projected the action. There were five rows

drum, raises her arms skywards and disappears in a flash of smoke before emerging seconds later in the middle of the crowd, where she is borne aloft on the shoulders of four strapping lads, Cleopatra-style, for a triumphant tour through a field of thousands of frantically waving arms, each reaching out to try and grab a piece of her.

Above and above right

On stage with plenty of bangs, pops and fizzes. Those who said Shania couldn't cut it live are force-fed double helpings of humble pie.

of computerised spotlights, three panning searchlights, 60-plus speakers hanging from the rigging to give it plenty of oomph and enough bangs, pops and fizzes to make you think Chinese New Year had come early. It was pure rock theatre on a scale that Metallica or the Rolling Stones might recognise. As part of the finale, during a rousing '(If You're Not In It For Love) I'm Outta Here!' she even steps onto a bass

Yes, the audiences loved her. They really loved their Shania. And none more so than the people of Timmins, Ontario. On Canada Day (1 July) 1999, she again returned to the town; this time to play the biggest concert the place had ever seen, with pyrotechnics and everything. Weeks beforehand, shops and homes had been displaying placards welcoming her home. She had even spent a few days beforehand walking and camping nearby in the woods she knew so well. The fact that it rained on the night didn't matter. Twenty thousand people were there in Hollinger Park to help celebrate. 'This is a perfect, perfect evening,' she told the crowd. Right there, right then she was on top of the world. And it felt good.

Selling stacks of records is one thing but, as any performer will tell you, there's nothing quite like the instant adrenaline high of having an adoring crowd eating out of your hand. And if there were ever any doubts in her own mind that she might somehow fail to live up to her fans' expectations, those were now firmly blown away. What's more, her detractors, who had insisted that Shania was simply a glossy studio creation, were forced to eat a large slice of humble pie. Live onstage, she proved herself to be right at home, a cheerleading bundle of limitless energy who works her socks off and who knows she's got exactly what it takes; voice, personality and looks all coming together in one powerful 5'4" package.

As Shania herself would be the first to admit, she is no vocal ballerina in the Mariah Carey mould, nor can she pin you helpless to the wall like fellow Canadian Celine Dion. What she does have, though, is an unlimited supply of unaffected warmth,

Above 'Taxi!' Shania plans a quick getaway to escape the attentions of over-enthusiastic fans.

an inclusive sense of fun and a simple desire to entertain, putting on the best show she possibly can. When she declares, 'It's as exciting as I always dreamed it would be. It's never tiring. I never get bored when I go out there on stage. I do the same songs every night – and I love it *every* night,' you know she is telling the truth; ever since she was a tot, it's all she ever wanted to do. What she

'My goal is to appeal to as many people I can. I'm not looking to leave country, but I do want to have more international success. The more people who hear your music the more satisfied you are as an artist.'

Far right In full regal mode and feeling like a woman, no doubt. Shania attends another award ceremony on her own while Mutt stays home polishing the gold discs.

has also got, of course, are the songs – her very own ones that everybody knows. And not just the odd hit single and a lot of padding, mind. 'When', 'You've Got A Way', 'Don't Be Stupid (You Know I Love You)', 'From This Moment On' and the rest are all known virtually inside out. Small wonder that her shows should have such a celebratory air to them. From moist-eyed ballads to toe-tapping rockers, it's like being plugged straight into a jukebox.

What applies to North America, however, doesn't automatically work in the rest of the global marketplace. Country music, in particular, with its corny image of stetsons and lariats, has always been a notoriously poor traveller; a minority taste at best with a lowbrow, strictly blue-collar reputation and not an ounce of cool. Just ask Garth Brooks, the most successful recording artist in the whole history of Nashville, who has never got much past first base on the rest of the planet. Shania's response to that bare fact was typically pragmatic: on home turf she would primarily be a country performer, while elsewhere around the globe she would be marketed as an all-purpose pop star. 'My goal is to appeal to as many people I can. I'm not looking to leave country, but I do want to have more international success. The more people who hear your music, the more satisfied you are as an artist,' she said.

The upshot of this was that *Come On Over* was subtly remodelled for the international audience. Offending steel guitars and fiddles were pushed further down into the mix, 'From This Moment On' was treated as a solo turn rather than a duet with Bryan White as on the original, and the cover photo was amended too, portraying the singer in a glamorous, silvery, bare-shouldered little number rather than an open-necked red blouse. Not that these changes signalled overnight success, especially not in the UK, where it would take nearly 18 months for the full Shania effect to really take hold and where she was still very much an unknown quantity, *The Woman In Me* having caused barely a ripple of interest, despite its multi-platinum standing across the Atlantic. Too country, wasn't she?

The UK campaign started in earnest with the release of 'You're Still The One' in February 1998, giving Shania her first Top Ten single and a passport into the world's most notoriously fickle record-buying market. 'When' and 'From This Moment On' followed later in the year, hitting numbers 18 and nine in the charts respectively. It was a start, but she was still a long way from household name status. At first, *Come On Over*, released in March 1998, performed equally soundly, getting to number 15 in the album charts, without ever suggesting it was likely to mount a serious challenge to that year's biggest winners, Robbie Williams and Ireland's The Corrs. During the summer there followed a brief but show-stealing performance before a 100,000 crowd in London's Hyde Park at the first Party In The Park and a short UK arena tour, both certainly helping to raise awareness a

'I write with comic relief. You can't take it seriously. I don't think hardcore country fans realise it, but everyone else knows that the songs are meant to be humorous and corny.'

notch or two. Yet by Christmas time, the album appeared to have run its course, having long slipped out of the bestseller lists. Shania's attempt to capture British hearts and wallets looked as if it was going to have to be put on hold for a while.

Come On Over, though, is no ordinary record. With 16 strong and varied tracks to choose from, it's a virtual stand-alone hit machine. Further proof of this came when 'From This Moment On' became the album's fourth UK hit single, reaching number nine. Lift-off was really achieved, however, at the beginning of May 1999, when 'That Don't Impress Me Much' was let loose, an irrepressible bit of fluff with its tongue planted firmly in its perfectly proportioned cheek. As Shania told *FHM* magazine, 'I write with comic relief. You can't take it seriously. I don't think hardcore country fans realise it, but everyone else knows that the songs are meant to be humorous and corny.' Well, hooray for that.

As ever, the video played a more than ample part in getting the song across to a wider public. This time Shania was a strawberry blonde with a slashed crimson mouth who's dressed top to toe (famous midriff excepted, of course) in leopardskin and who just happens to be hitchhiking her way across the Southern Californian desert. (Don't ask.) Guys with a variety of

throbbing, wheeled machinery at their disposal, not forgetting the Lawrence of Arabia hunk on a rearing black charger, stop to offer her a lift. She looks them up. She looks them down. She waves them all on their way. Not even buff Brad Pitt would make the grade, she tells us with a wink. It was fun, sexy, stylish, about as country as downtown Manhattan and it obviously struck a whopping chord. A favourite with both MTV and senior sibling VH-1, it hung

Above The choice is yours: slinky crocheted little number or old string vest? Either way, Shania letting rip one more time.

Far left White top, black bra: always a tricky one. Shania pushes the sartorial envelope for a London audience, July 1999.

started shifting copies all over again, more quickly than before. By September it had reached the top of the perch, further aided by another tour, some judicious TV slots and 'Man! I Feel Like A Woman!' hitting the shops, accompanied by another visually irresistible video: a nod-and-a-wink spoof of Robert Palmer's 'Addicted To Love', with Shania fronting a band of smouldering male models and stripping down to dominatrix thigh boots and the miniest of minis – only the whip seemed to be missing. This was definitely one for the lads, whichever way you interpreted her avowed lyrical intent to occasionally misbehave and forget she's a 'lady'. As hardline feminists shuddered at the duplicity, everybody else rather enjoyed the sight and sound of a woman in her prime apparently calling the shots. Either way, the album quickly made up for lost time; going on to become 1999's biggest UK seller; two million-plus and still going strong after a couple of years. No doubt about it, she had definitely arrived now.

The year meant more industry awards too. At the Grammys, felicitously crammed into her strictest 'Man! I Feel Like A Woman' disciplinarian gear, Shania picked up awards for Country Song and Country Female Vocal Of The Year for 'You're Still The One'. Mutt, as ever, was nowhere to be seen. 'He never comes to these things with

around the UK Top Ten for almost three months, sold over 600,000 copies and became the single most-played track on British radio during 1999 (46,371 plays, according to monitoring outfit Music Control; how do they count these things?), easily shoving Madonna's 'Beautiful Stranger' into second spot.

'That Don't Impress Me Much' was just the boost that *Come On Over* needed. It me,' she trotted out for the thousandth time. 'I don't think you'll ever see him with me. He's just a behind-the-scenes kind of guy. If he wants to get dressed up, it's to go to dinner or to be entertained, not to be the focus of attention. He doesn't pay too much attention to the awards. He's just really happy things are going as well as they are, so we're really happy as a team.'

The Twain/Lange team had another reason to be cheerful in September when, finally, Nashville cracked, Shania picking up the highly prestigious Entertainer Of The Year Award at the annual Country Music Association bash. 'Well, Shania, that ought to shut everybody up. You did it, baby!' emcee and fellow country star Vince Gill told the crowd and the millions of people watching at home on TV. Nobody was in any doubt what he meant, least of all the singer herself. 'Well, I'm not just a lap dancer, after all,' she could afford to chuckle backstage after the ceremony.

In accepting the award from country star and her own former champion Reba McEntire, capping what had been an extraordinary five years, Shania became the first woman since McEntire herself to scoop the honour thirteen years earlier. Maybe not the way that some people had wanted or expected, but she had definitely done it. 'My roots are Dolly Parton, Merle Haggard,

Waylon Jennings, and that's never going to change,' she explained to *Country Music People* magazine. 'But we change. We evolve. We grow and create music of our own – we come into our own. And I'm into whoever I am right now. I'm enjoying it. I'm happy fans are enjoying it. And I think this honour comes mostly as a surprise because I sort of convinced myself that I wasn't going to win a thing.'

Above Recognition at last from the Country Music Association as 1999's Entertainer Of The Year, topping off what had been an extraordinary, record-breaking five years for the Canadian.

'I don't like bad attention. I like good attention. I'm no different than anyone else.'

Far right Las Vegas, January 2000 and Shania is now top of the tree, the biggest female singing star on the planet. Not a bad result for the girl from little old Timmins, Ontario, is it? Expect plenty more to follow.

And as *Come On Over* steadfastly refused to drop out of the charts, Shania keeps on winning; she is already into uncharted territory for a female performer, officially being the first woman to notch up US sales in excess of ten million for back-to-back albums. Indeed, its enduring success has given her that rarest of luxuries – time. With singles like 'You've Got A Way', 'Don't Be Stupid (You Know I Love You)' and Tipper Gore's favourite 'Rock This Country!' continuing to be successfully plucked from it, there became no need for her to rush back to the studio to record a hasty follow-up. She could afford to pace herself and her future career. And everything points to her being around for the duration.

Already, it seems, a proposed album of Christmas songs (what an old romantic she is), originally pencilled in to coincide with 1999's festivities, has been put back a year. As for that much-anticipated fourth album proper, who knows? Late 2000? Early 2001? What you can safely bet your house on is that when it does appear the timing and contents will be absolutely right, calculated to the nth degree, just like everything else bearing her name since *The Woman In Me* took off. Besides, Shania's hubbie and musical partner, Mutt, has been more than quietly keeping himself busy of late, working with America's current champion boy band, the Backstreet Boys; their *Millennium* album just happening to be 1999's biggest US seller. With that continuing Midas touch to call on, how can she possibly fail to come up with the goods again?

By rights, boredom and burnout, both for Shania and the rest of us, should have set in long ago. She knows it too, hence the lower profile of late. Yet she has now achieved that rarefied level of stardom and celebrity where even the very act of doing nothing invites speculation and makes news, including her declaration that she would effectively be taking the year 2000 off. So when Shania goes to the theatre in London with her husband, that's in the press the next day. Shania helping to write songs for Britney Spears?

Better put that in too. In the absence of anything new, any old scraps will do. And modern appetites can be voracious. It's madness, of course, but what can you do? Besides, having played the media game so expertly, she can hardly complain now. Nor does she, not really: 'You know what it is. We're all very selfish people. We love the attention when it's complimentary and we hate the attention when it sucks. I don't like bad attention. I like good attention. I'm no different than anyone else.'

That's a recurring theme for Shania: that despite being rich, famous, blessed with cover-girl looks and now living away from the hustle and bustle in a nineteenth-century Swiss manor house with Sophia Loren, Tina Turner and Phil Collins for neighbours, she's no different from the rest of us. The trappings may have changed, there may be plenty of dollars in the kitty, but in her mind she is much the same as she ever was: just a little old singer from Timmins, Ontario, who has had her fair share of downs as well as ups and happens to have made it through to the land of milk and honey on the other side. It might be a myth, but it's a beguiling one: Shania is still just a country girl at heart.

Discography

ALBUMS

(Chart placings as per Billboard Country Albums Chart: peak position)

Shania Twain (1993)	68
The Woman In Me (1995)	1
Come On Over (1997)	1

SINGLES

(Chart placings as per Billboard Hot Country Singles Chart: peak position)

What Made You Say That (1993)	55
Dance With The One That Brought You (1993)	55
You Lay A Whole Lot Of Love On Me (1993)	59
Whose Bed Have Your Boots Been Under? (1995)	11
Any Man Of Mine (1995)	5
The Woman In Me (Needs The Man In You) (1995)	26
(If You're Not In It For Love) I'm Outta Here!(1995)	1
You Win My Love (1996)	1
No One Needs To Know (1996)	1
Home Ain't Where His Heart Is (Anymore) (1996)	15
God Bless The Child (1996)	48
Love Gets Me Every Time (1997)	1
Don't Be Stupid (You Know I Love You) (1997)	6
You're Still The One (1998)	1
From This Moment On (1998)	6
Honey, I'm Home (1998)	1
That Don't Impress Me Much (1999)	8
Man! I Feel Like A Woman! (1999)	4
You've Got A Way (1999)	13
Come On Over (1999)	6
Rock This Country (2000)	3

Index

First published in the United States of America by
Unanimous Ltd
254–258 Goswell Road
London, England EC1V 7RL

ISBN: 1–56649–136–3

Distributed by Welcome Rain Distribution LLC

Editor: Nicola Birtwisle
Design: Staziker Jones

Printed in Italy

Picture credits

Big Pictures p50; Country Music Association/Chris Hollo pp36, 91; LFI pp4, 13, 24, 28, 55, 58, 84 right, 87, 88; Liaison pp8, 16, 22, 25, 26, 34, 35, 38, 46, 53, 61, 72, 76, 81; Mapart Publishing p18; Pictorial Press pp33, 78; Redferns pp1, 2, 9, 10, 12, 20, 30, 31, 40, 42, 43, 44, 48 top left, 49, 63, 64, 68, 69, 85; Retna pp6, 19, 23, 32, 37, 45, 48 bottom left, 54, 57, 65, 67, 70, 73 left, 75, 77, 79, 82, 84 left, 89, 93; Frank Spooner pp15, 27, 52, 90; Toronto Star pp21, 66.